PROJECT-BASED LEARNING+

GRADES 6–12

This book is dedicated to the loving memory of my stepfather,
Thoms Francis Reddington.
Where the ocean meets the sky, you'll be sailing.

PROJECT-BASED LEARNING+

GRADES 6–12

Enhancing Academic, Social, and Emotional Learning

Jorge Valenzuela

Foreword by Yaritza Villalba

FOR INFORMATION:

Corwin

A SAGE Company

2455 Teller Road

Thousand Oaks, California 91320

(800) 233-9936

www.corwin.com

SAGE Publications Ltd.

1 Oliver's Yard

55 City Road

London EC1Y 1SP

United Kingdom

SAGE Publications India Pvt. Ltd.

Unit No 323-333, Third Floor, F-Block

International Trade Tower Nehru Place

New Delhi 110 019

SAGE Publications Asia-Pacific Pte. Ltd.

18 Cross Street #10-10/11/12

China Square Central

Singapore 048423

Vice President and
  Editorial Director: Monica Eckman

Publisher: Jessica Allan

Content Development Editor: Mia Rodriguez

Senior Editorial Assistant: Natalie Delpino

Editorial Intern: Lex Nunez

Production Editor: Tori Mirsadjadi

Copy Editor: Integra

Typesetter: C&M Digitals (P) Ltd.

Proofreader: Sarah J. Duffy

Cover Designer: Scott Van Atta

Marketing Manager: Olivia Bartlett

Printed in Canada

Library of Congress Cataloging-in-Publication Data

Names: Valenzuela, Jorge (Engineering teacher) author.

Title: Project based learning+, grades 6-12 : a framework for implementing academic, social, and emotional learning/Jorge Valenzuela.

Other titles: Project based learning plus, grades 6-12

Description: Thousand Oaks, California : Corwin, [2024] | Includes bibliographical references and index.

Identifiers: LCCN 2023016911 | ISBN 9781071889169 (paperback) | ISBN 9781071889176 (epub) | ISBN 9781071889206 (epub) | ISBN 9781071889183 (pdf)

Subjects: LCSH: Project method in teaching. | Affective education. | Social learning.

Classification: LCC LB1027.43 .V35 2024 | DDC 371.3/6—dc23/eng/20230517
LC record available at https://lccn.loc.gov/2023016911

This book is printed on acid-free paper.

23 24 25 26 27 10 9 8 7 6 5 4 3 2 1

DISCLAIMER: This book may direct you to access third-party content via web links, QR codes, or other scannable technologies, which are provided for your reference by the author(s). Corwin makes no guarantee that such third-party content will be available for your use and encourages you to review the terms and conditions of such third-party content. Corwin takes no responsibility and assumes no liability for your use of any third-party content, nor does Corwin approve, sponsor, endorse, verify, or certify such third-party content.

CONTENTS

Visit the companion website at
resources.corwin.com/ProjectBasedLearning+
for downloadable resources.

Note From the Publisher: The author has provided video and web content throughout the book that is available to you through QR (quick response) codes. To read a QR code, you must have a smartphone or tablet with a camera. We recommend that you download a QR code reader app that is made specifically for your phone or tablet brand.

FOREWORD

By Yaritza Villalba

What are the core elements of high-quality project-based learning (PBL)? What are the components of social and emotional learning (SEL)? Why is it important for educators to understand how both PBL and SEL are necessary for the success of all students and educators? Jorge Valenzuela has developed this remarkable framework to answer these questions and many more. The PBL+ Framework supplies resources and effective strategies to support every educator in adopting effective equitable practices for the success of all learners.

In answering these questions and supplying a guide for the successful implementation of strategies, Jorge reminds us of the importance of creating opportunities for students to problem-solve and make real-world connections to their learnings. PBL is all about creating student-centered performance tasks that enable students to work collaboratively while also being aware of the skills necessary to contribute to a learning environment in and out of the classroom.

In this framework, Jorge encourages educators to use their knowledge of students to guide their pedagogical practices. In doing so, he reminds us of the importance of knowledge of self and others and the benefits of using this knowledge to improve learning outcomes and create a space of intellectual prosperity for all. Schools should be spaces for students to thrive and where educators use culturally responsive sustaining strategies to meet students' individual needs through curriculum, building community with families, and developing lesson tasks that are reflective of each student and their prior experiences.

How are you preparing to serve the students in your school building? With the PBL+ Framework, Jorge offers insight into the impact that empathy and relevancy have on student performance. He breaks down core instructional practices that are relevant to K–12 education and beyond. By identifying skills, performance tasks, and driving questions, he equips educators with tools for success. This book is designed for all educators who are looking for ways to supply effective and sustaining pedagogy.

Jorge provides the perfect guide, with examples for each educator and diverse learning environments. He believes that all students should be given the opportunity to be their best selves, and throughout this book you will find gems that spark curiosity, agreeance, and the desire to continue reading on to discover new ways to build a culture of learning, despite all the challenges in education, many of which were exposed by the COVID-19 pandemic. With education facing difficulties, many are challenged by finding strategies that enhance student learning while stimulating interests. We must search for the answers that supply actionable strategies for us to educate and learn alongside our students. For historically marginalized students, PBL tasks serve as a bridge that connects content to relevancy. Schools must cultivate environments for learning and encourage students to critically think beyond the content being presented. This is what Jorge is supplying in this book.

To provide students with effective learning outcomes, you must believe that the strategies are attainable. I recognize that learning new ways of teaching and learning may be difficult, but Jorge supplies bite-sized practices that will intensify your pedagogical skills.

If you are searching for a guide that will restore your faith in the impact that supplying multiple entry points into a lesson, unit, or curriculum has on students, you have found it! This guide is significant to education; it empowers educators to look beyond test scores and supply ways for students to learn that are beyond recalling information. Jorge aligns tasks to Common Core State Standards (CCSS), SEL, and research-based strategies to engage all learners, regardless of their grade level.

In *Project-Based Learning+*, Jorge is giving educators and schools the tools to aid students. All schools and districts will receive help from this toolkit, which is designed to build community among all stakeholders in the learning process and innovate and cultivate opportunities for growth. With this book's help, you can begin your journey of growth and ensure that all your students' needs are heard and met.

ACKNOWLEDGMENTS

I want to personally thank God for grace and faith, my parents, Mariam, Anisa, Daniel, and Graham.

I want to express my deepest gratitude to my dear friends, Jenni and Jemma Deskins, Shelby Giles, Phil Bristol, Elizabeth Peña, Al Jackson, Steve Brown, Tongilere Roache, Erica Coleman, and Wanda Mclean, for their unwavering support and encouragement throughout my writing journey.

Thank you, Tom Berger, Marva Hinton, Rhonda Simley, Kenneth Nance Michael Courtney, Aaron Monroe, Dr. Randall Johnson, Dr. Stanley Jones, Dr. Kelvin Edwards, Dr. Marcus Newsome, Drew Hirshon, Laurel Byrd, Sylvia Escobar, Erin Salberg, Shaina Victoria Glass, Jason Bohrer, Yaritza Villalba, Coach Victor Hicks, Victoria Thompson, Diana Fingal, Dr. Crystal Caballero, Dr. Krista Leh, Ezekiel Valenga, James Fester, Katrina Futrell, Michelle Moore, Tre' Gammage, Melissa Campesi, Breauna Hall, Chanel Johnson, Brad Sever, Dr. Evisha Ford, and Dr. Sheldon Eakins for collaborating and adding to me professionally.

The development of the PBL+ Framework and the creation of this book were made possible by the invaluable contributions of the hundreds of teachers I met while coaching PBL through numerous workshops and data collections. I am also grateful for the support of Corwin, Sonja Hollins-Alexander, Lydia Chavira, the schools I partner with, and the publishing team of Mia Rodriguez, Lucas Schleicher, Natalie Delpino, Ricardo Ramirez, and Jessica Allan.

A VERY SPECIAL ACKNOWLEDGMENT

I am expressing my deepest gratitude to Dr. Serbrenia Sims for always believing in me and being a collaborative partner in my work and throughout my doctoral program. I would not have achieved several milestones without her support and encouragement. Thank you, Dr. Sims, for your invaluable contributions to my success!

IMPORTANT MENTIONS

PBL and SEL have much overlap but are also incredibly diverse and far-ranging topics and pedagogies; so much so that deep understanding requires learning from more than one person or organization. I want to thank and acknowledge the following scholars and entities for their fantastic contributions to these spaces.

The Collaborative for Academic, Social, and Emotional Learning (CASEL); Corwin; Edutopia; the Association for Supervision and Curriculum Development (ACSD); the International Society for Technology in Education (ISTE); Solution Tree; Defined Learning; EL Education; Tre' Gammage; PBLWorks; and countless others.

I also credit the works of other notable authors, artists, and life and education coaches like Eckhart Tolle, Travis Bradberry, Jay McTighe, John Hattie, Ron Berger, Don Miguel Ruiz, Dr. Stephen R. Covey, Malcolm Gladwell, Ava DuVernay, Curtis "50 Cent" Jackson, and Tim Grover for helping to shape my insights.

ABOUT THE AUTHOR

Jorge Valenzuela is a highly regarded performance and education coach, author, and speaker at Lifelong Learning Defined. He got his start in education and has helped countless educators improve their leadership and instructional innovation skills. Jorge specializes in emphasizing core instruction and is a trusted deliverer of reputable professional training in team building, project-based learning, STEM pathways, and SEL integration across the curriculum. He partners with superintendents and provides professional development on behalf of ASCD, Corwin, Instructional Innovation Partners, and Solution Tree. He has authored several books and is the host of the Lifelong Learning Defined podcast.

Jorge has a Bachelor of Science in management information systems from SUNY Old Westbury in New York and a master's in school administration and supervision from Phoenix University. He is currently fulfilling the requirements for his doctoral degree at Old Dominion University.

INTRODUCTION

> *Before proceeding with anything new in your classroom, always ask yourself, what do the kids I teach need?*
>
> —Tony Casipit
> Technology and Engineering Educator

As both a teacher and instructional coach, the most critical question I am trying to answer and help others answer is "What do the kids I teach need?" Because students and school contexts vary, so do the answers. They are unique—even for the same kid or groups of kids on a different day. I think "What do the kids I teach need?" should be the most urgent question both individual teachers and school-based teaching teams need to ponder and figure out to develop positive interpersonal relationships with their students and for making the instructional decisions necessary to help them blossom into better people and learners. Some might say that's a tall task for educators, especially nowadays when many are teaching through trauma and crises in post-COVID classrooms (Mason, 2021). I can relate and empathize.

This book doesn't shy away from the problematic issues teachers face in their classrooms. It was written to assist teachers in teaching post-pandemic learners and beyond using a research-informed framework for improving teaching using project-based learning (PBL) and helping them develop emotional intelligence (EQ) skills through social and emotional learning (SEL). On the one hand, PBL is a research-based instructional approach teachers can use to engage learners over an extended period to solve compelling problems they care about and acquire the skills and dispositions needed for successful lives. On the other hand, SEL is an educational approach designed to assist kids with developing their EQ skills to help anchor their learning process and decisions within school curricula. Both PBL and SEL are pedagogies that have been proven to meet the academic and social needs of students (Lucas Education Research [LER], 2021). I believe implementing PBL and SEL in post-COVID classrooms effectively can also have positive effects on educators too—the second part of this book therefore focuses on uplifting SEL competencies in our PBL teaching plans.

THE IMPACT OF COVID ON TEACHERS

Before diving deeper into PBL and SEL, I want to acknowledge some of the problems facing our teachers and profession. Teaching post-COVID is difficult—the pandemic wreaked havoc on public education and exposed academic and social inequities (Dorn et al., 2020), causing many to question and leave our profession (Kurtz, 2022). Results from a survey conducted by the EdWeek Research Center are bleak and tell us the following (Kurtz, 2022):

- More than 40% of the teachers surveyed reported they were "likely to leave the profession in the next two years."

- Only 44% reported they were "treated like professionals by the public."

- Less than 15% reported they were "very satisfied with [their] jobs."

Additionally, here are some of the challenges expressed by teachers in their own words from a survey by the Christensen Institute (2021):

- "Student behavior is a huge problem. I spend more time redirecting than presenting instruction. Many students have learned non-school practices that make it difficult to create a high functioning independent learning environment."

- "I have students who need extra support for social-emotional learning. I don't have enough resources and time to meet and talk with them."

- "Most teachers feel like zombies just going through the motions of the day."

- "The workload is unreal. The pressure on teachers during this time is more than ever before." (pp. 14, 15)

After reading the abovementioned quotes, I cannot in good conscience overlook the plight of our teachers or not attempt to address some of their concerns in this book. Moreover, administrators need to rally teachers in ways that don't seem disingenuous or have an agenda to have them comply. That said, school leaders must consider the best ways of supporting their teachers who are staying in the profession by choice and new colleagues entering a potentially tricky new job situation (Valenzuela, 2022f).

Systems were broken pre-pandemic (Barrington, 2022), and now our teachers know it and rightly refuse to be blamed. There are no easy answers, but for those remaining, we have to take better care of ourselves in and out of the schoolhouse. A silver lining of the pandemic is that it has ensured personal wellness is here to stay (Cal State East Bay, 2022); for many, it's become an exigent priority. Managing our needs with those of students is a balance that all educators need to make consciously; otherwise, we may be leaving too much to chance in our lives and the classroom. Even individuals outside of education must manage their needs in tandem with those they serve (Ahmed, 2021). From business owners, accountants, lawyers, florists, designers, retail workers, family members, and everyone in between, it's not easy but definitely worth exploring. The SEL-infused PBL methodology introduced in this book can help us put practice to that exploration.

MY DISCOVERY OF PROJECT-BASED LEARNING

I first became aware of PBL in 2013 when my colleagues on the curriculum and instruction (C&I) team at Richmond Public Schools, in Virginia, and I explored the best teaching methods for hands-on learning in our district. Colleagues from another school system suggested we try our hand at PBL. Unfortunately, at that time, it was difficult to find local training or anyone who was grounded in the pedagogy of PBL, so our progress stalled momentarily. Later, in 2014, I attended the Association for Career and Technical Education (ACTE) conference in Nashville, Tennessee. At the conference, I attended my first presentation on PBL and was introduced to the Buck Institute for Education, the then world leader for PBL methodology and resources. I left the ACTE conference inspired and wanting to learn how to implement PBL well in my school district. I requested my supervisor to allow me to attend PBL World—the nation's premier annual PBL event hosted by the Buck Institute (PBLWorks, 2022). Although I didn't make it to PBL World, I became accepted into the Buck Institute's national faculty development program, where I learned PBL and how to implement it across various educational contexts.

Since 2014, I've spent most of the last decade touring the United States (30 states and 70+ cities), working with K–16 schools to help them understand and implement PBL across the curriculum. Part of the work is to coach educators through developing PBL units they can immediately implement in their classrooms. Through lots of travel, my PBL work opened my eyes to the instructional needs of teachers and how PBL can be used to boost their teaching in urban, rural, big-city, and small-town settings for multitudes of learners with diverse needs. This became glaring on my return visits to many schools and localities for follow-up support to the initial PBL training. Seeing countless teachers become more confident planners and practitioners in their classrooms and tangible artifacts evidencing student work increased my confidence in my coaching and strengthened my message to schools.

Data collection was, and continues to be, a significant part of this work because it helps inform and tweak practice. I have learned a lot from my participants—they are trusted partners often dictating how I plan and facilitate sessions. I have found that all teachers need a trusted set of pedagogical strategies supported by tools and frameworks at their disposal. They also need to confidently reach for those tools as students and times change—pivoting with ease, comfort, and knowing they are making instructional decisions that provide their students the proper support. In my own teaching evolution, I have gleaned insights from several practices and pedagogies. I don't see PBL as the only way to teach. Instead, PBL can be a powerful approach when coupled with SEL and high-yielding strategies showing high influences on student achievement and engagement and applied correctly to define an empowering student experience.

WHY WE NEED A PBL+ FRAMEWORK

Using data to inform my work with teachers is critical. It has informed me that for teachers to feel confident using PBL in their classroom, they need to understand what PBL is, learn ways to boost their learners' EQ, know the students they serve, and adapt practical strategies for planning and facilitating PBL using strategies with high influences on student engagement and achievement.

The PBL+ Framework provides educators guidance for strengthening their PBL journey and refining their instructional practice over time. Each component of the framework is supported by research and is grounded in practical steps that are replicable in any classroom. The aim is to make PBL accessible for every educator by providing them with strategies for getting started either independently or with colleagues—ideally, within a grade-level teaching team servicing the same students.

Moreover, the components in the framework consider that not all educators teach in districts where PBL training is readily available. Even when training is available, critical next steps and additional coaching required for improving practice may not be. To adequately support readers, each element in the framework has a dedicated chapter in the forthcoming pages explaining its relevance, research, and implementation strategies. Here are the elements in the framework:

1. Understand the components of research-informed PBL

2. Understand the basics of the CASEL 5 (for SEL) and emotional intelligence

3. Use knowledge of students to inform teaching

4. Design projects relevant to the students you serve

5. Use frequent feedback cycles to guide student work

WHO SHOULD READ THIS BOOK?

This book is written for K–12 teachers who are looking to develop or enhance their teaching using PBL but may not have experience aligning PBL to SEL and other related strategies needed for making sound and calculated instructional decisions. That's where the PBL+ Framework can help. This book is also for instructional leaders looking to implement PBL across the curriculum in their schools using data-driven high-leverage and tangible steps that improve instruction. This book can be a manual for schools and educators looking to raise equity for vulnerable students by intentionally using PBL to activate SEL in projects but who may be unsure of where to start. Through lessons on the fundamentals of PBL, SEL, and other equity-raising practices, both the novice and expert can level up their PBL teaching by applying the contents in this book.

Whether you're an English language arts (ELA), mathematics, science, history, art, computer science, or career and technical education (CTE) teacher, this book provides the know-how for strategically engaging your learners in projects while still maintaining the appropriate rigor levels required for your class. This book is also for the special education support teacher and teacher tasked to hold after-school learning experiences. Although you can adapt the material in this book independently, you should do so as part of a school's collaborative teaching team. Whether you are teaching students in a support role, in an after-school club, or just as a fun activity, you will find strategies in this book to support you on your PBL- and SEL-infused teaching journey.

HOW TO NAVIGATE THIS BOOK

This book is organized into three parts, each with three or more chapters.

Part 1 defines and explores the fundamentals of the PBL+ Framework and provides empirical evidence and many easy-to-replicate examples for its use as part of a comprehensive PBL teaching plan. Also, the intersection of educational equity, SEL, and sound teaching strategies is highlighted in these chapters through research, tools and frameworks, and practical advice. The five elements in the framework (and Chapters 1 through 5, respectively) are as follows.

Chapter 1, Element 1: Understand the Components of Research-Informed Project-Based Learning. In this chapter, we consider pacing and teaching structure for projects. We explore relevant research and prepare to implement essential elements to strengthen project ideas and create the best learning experiences for students.

Chapter 2, Element 2: Understand the Basics of the CASEL 5 (for SEL) and Emotional Intelligence. In this chapter, we explore the SEL competencies of the Collaborative for Academic, Social, and Emotional Learning (CASEL) and use tools to help kids develop emotional intelligence skills.

Chapter 3, Element 3: Use Knowledge of Students to Inform Teaching. In this chapter, we explore appropriate tools and methods to become better familiar with students so we can begin to make instructional decisions that accommodate their unique needs.

Chapter 4, Element 4: Design Projects Relevant to the Students You Serve. In this chapter, we explore and adapt a methodology for expanding project ideas using our curricular resources to design and fine-tune a personalized PBL unit to our class context.

Chapter 5, Element 5: Use Frequent Feedback Cycles to Guide Student Work. In this chapter, we cover assessment in PBL and learn to adapt a set of handy protocols for giving students feedback as they complete their products or performance tasks in drafts. This chapter also offers guidance on keeping project work at the appropriate rigor levels and grading individual student work during PBL units.

Part 2 provides K–12 teachers with dedicated chapters on adaptable projects uplifting the CASEL 5 competencies of self-awareness, self-management, social awareness, relationship management, and responsible decision making. Each chapter provides an overview of SEL competencies in alignment with PBL and strategies for adopting practices that integrate the CASEL 5 into PBL units. The chapters in Part 2 are as follows.

Chapter 6: Understanding Self-Awareness for Connecting Passion and Purpose. This chapter delves into the self-awareness and self-management SEL competencies and provides an adaptable PBL unit educators can personalize for their classroom along with recommendations for equitable implementation.

Chapter 7: Understanding Social Awareness for Having Successful Relationships. This chapter delves into the social awareness and relationship management SEL competencies and provides an adaptable PBL unit educators can personalize for their classroom along with recommendations for equitable implementation.

Chapter 8: Responsible Decision Making: From Awareness to Action. This chapter delves into the responsible decision-making SEL competency and provides an adaptable PBL unit educators can personalize for their classroom along with recommendations for equitable implementation.

Part 3 focuses on enhancing a PBL teaching plan with tools and resources that help learners work together with shared agreements and guidelines for fruitful collaboration. Strategies for maintaining your grade-level rigor levels and grading students in PBL are also addressed to help teachers effectively ensure learning and assess student work.

Chapter 9: Using a 5-Step Roadmap to Activate Student Engagement and Rigorous PBL This chapter helps teachers consider daily engagement in their teaching, prepare compelling and engaging entry events at the start of a PBL unit, and understand the steps needed for engagement throughout the entire project process. Downloadable and adaptable tools are also provided.

Chapter 10: Fostering Collaboration and Teamwork. This chapter helps teachers prepare students to collaborate and work on projects effectively through shared agreements and collaborative tools. Downloadable and adaptable tools are also provided.

Chapter 11: Helping Students Prepare for the Public Product. This chapter provides excellent guidelines and recommendations for preparing students to present their ideas, new learning, and calls to action in public presentations.

Finally, note that in each chapter, you will find *Important Note* feature boxes that highlight unique elements of a concept or strategy. I aim to supplement and clarify reader understanding throughout the book. Additionally, this book provides access to additional resources in the appendices, page 135. You can also visit the companion website at resources.corwin.com/ProjectBasedLearning+, where you can find downloadable versions of multiple templates shown throughout. Finally, we conclude our book with cited references and resources.

online resources

PART 1

THE PBL+ FRAMEWORK

The following five chapters offer readers an in-depth explanation of each element of the PBL+ Framework, research supporting each element, and recommendations for actionable and equitable classroom implementation practices. Furthermore, this section also provides recommended materials educators can use to improve their PBL teaching plan by focusing on equity and enhancing the emotional intelligence skillsets of their students through SEL.

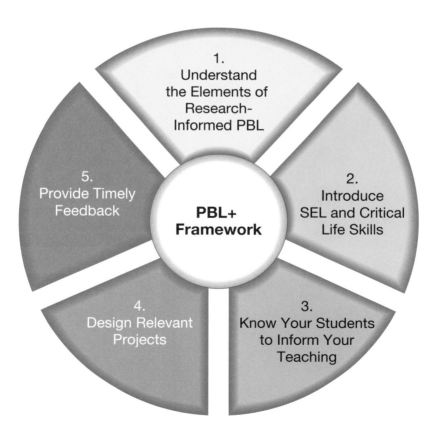

1. Understand the Elements of Research-Informed PBL

2. Introduce SEL and Critical Life Skills

3. Know Your Students to Inform Your Teaching

4. Design Relevant Projects

5. Provide Timely Feedback

PBL+ Framework

CHAPTER 1

ELEMENT 1: UNDERSTAND THE COMPONENTS OF RESEARCH-INFORMED PROJECT-BASED LEARNING

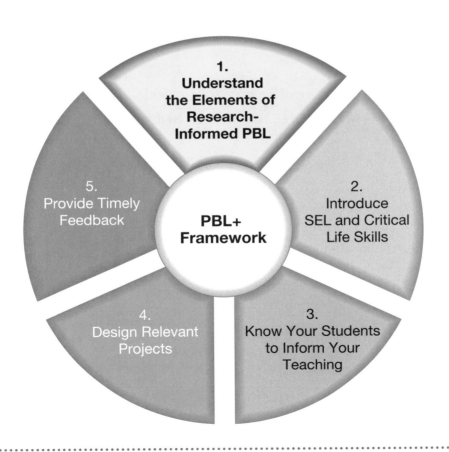

This chapter provides the foundational knowledge required for understanding research-informed project-based learning (PBL) and is an actionable guide for helping you define your students' PBL experience. We begin by making PBL accessible to all teachers by demystifying common PBL hurdles and providing practical recommendations for pacing and teaching structure that doesn't neglect academic rigor. We then explore recent research by Lucas Education Research showing that PBL is a proven effective teaching methodology in various educational contexts, including for historically underserved students.

To further provide PBL structure and guidelines, we delve into the elements of the High-Quality Project-Based Learning (HQPBL) framework. The HQPBL framework is Do-It-Yourself (DIY), research-based, and developed in consensus with PBL experts. This chapter will unpack this framework used in the project examples in Part 2 of this book. Furthermore, the concepts and tools uplifted in this chapter can be applied across any curriculum and are required to successfully implement the following elements in the PBL+ Framework.

LEARNING INTENTIONS

▶ Readers will be able to

- accurately define projects,
- confront common PBL hurdles,
- review research that supports PBL in various educational contexts,
- understand the six elements in the HQPBL framework and how they define the student experience, and
- develop the multiple skillsets associated with each of the HQPBL elements.

When we say projects, what exactly do we mean? This is an important question that I've asked participants at the very beginning of our PBL workshops for years. Teachers need to understand the instructional approach they're attempting to use. Take a moment to answer it yourself—write it down if you'd like. Responses to this question vary from person to person, and many say a variation of the following:

- Real-world learning and application
- Kids working together to create something useful
- Learners solving an open-ended problem
- Authentic learning experiences

If your answer(s) included any of the above, you're definitely on the right path. But there are a few things I want you to consider as you delve into the content in this book and plan to facilitate your own projects with students. *Project-based learning is a research-based instructional approach teachers can use to engage learners over an extended period to solve compelling real-world problems and acquire the skills and dispositions needed for successful lives.* Although there's a lot you can glean from this definition of PBL, here are two critical things I want you to genuinely consider as you reflect on your identity as a PBL teacher or coach:

1. PBL is a research-based instructional approach—a teaching methodology—a way to teach that has been proven to impact student learning and achievement positively (Lucas Education Research [LER], n.d.-a).

2. Learners will need to engage in projects over an extended period. This means that intended learning in projects doesn't occur in one or two days—that's because kids need to engage in intellectual challenges to explore new concepts and skills, wrestle with ideas, and present solutions to an authentic audience. This will take time. Two to three weeks tops is a suitable amount of time for a high-quality project.

If you're like most teachers or me, the abovementioned two items will bring you comfort and probably some discomfort too. On the one hand, many find comfort in knowing they are attempting to implement a valuable approach to learning which will require some time for young people to master. On the other hand, where do I begin with all of this? If that's your primary concern—no worries. It takes time to master facilitating PBL well for students. This book provides the playbook leveraging evidence for PBL with diverse student populations and research-informed frameworks and tools you'll need to begin and take your PBL coaching to the level you want to achieve.

USING EVIDENCE TO IMPROVE PBL PRACTICE

PBL is a constructivist teaching approach. Constructivist teaching says that learning occurs when learners actively engage in knowledge construction and the learning process to make deep meaning and connections to other branches of knowledge (A. Gray, n.d.). Constructivism is a paradigm for teaching and learning and is an amalgamation of the behavioral and cognitive learning theories and also shows up in other theories like general systems theory and communications theory (Valenzuela, 2019c).

As elements of constructivism inform the theory for PBL, PBL practitioners should understand why and how such practices help students learn along with ways of leveling up their own PBL teaching practices to enhance the experience of their learners. As we begin to test and evaluate what works in our classroom, having a trusted source for getting our knowledge is critical. If you're unsure where to go or how to start unpacking the right resources—here are some recommendations that guide my own PBL action research.

Lucas Education Research is the research arm of the George Lucas Educational Foundation (LER, n.d.-b) and a trusted source for PBL research. For the past 30 years, the foundation has worked to transform education—including a niched design-based research approach focused on teachers' needs and participation in a variety of education settings targeting and showing positive impacts on student achievement in science, social studies, social and emotional learning (SEL), literacy, numeracy, and advanced placement (AP) by using PBL. In 2021, Lucas Education Research published six research briefs summarizing the findings of peer-reviewed studies examining the impact of PBL across disciplines and grade levels (LER, 2021). Insights gleaned from the briefs can be used to help education stakeholders improve their understanding of new empirical evidence uplifting the effectiveness of PBL to learners with diverse needs (including the underserved) and across multiple academic settings.

Here are some of the most significant findings from the research brief titled *Rigorous Project-Based Learning Is a Powerful Lever for Improving Equity* (LER, 2021)—along with data points that make a powerful case for using PBL, including for students at risk of academic failure due to socioeconomic challenges and attending low-performing schools. It's important to note that the research brief discusses findings from four recent and rigorous studies.

- Integrating PBL in AP US Government and Politics and Environmental Science courses increased the probability of students achieving a passing score on AP exams by about eight percentage points in the first year and ten percentage points after teachers had two years of experience teaching high-quality PBL units (Saavedra et al., 2021).

- Middle school students in high-poverty, diverse California schools that learned science with PBL outperformed peers who received traditional instruction by 11 percentage points on science testing. They also made achievement gains on the state's end-of-year math and English language arts assessments (Deutscher et al., 2021).

- Using PBL, English learners from low-income families outperformed peers on a language proficiency test (Deutscher et al., 2021).

- Third-grade students in Michigan engaged in an interdisciplinary project-based science curriculum performed eight percentage points better on a key science assessment than peers receiving traditional instruction. Additionally, the positive effect of PBL on academic achievement held across racial and ethnic groups and socioeconomic levels regardless of prior reading proficiency—showing that struggling readers outperformed struggling readers receiving traditional instruction (Krajcik et al., 2021).

- Second-grade Michigan students in low-income, low-performing schools learning social studies and literacy in a project-based curriculum achieved five to six more months of learning gains in social studies and two to three more months in informational reading than peers receiving traditional instruction (Duke et al., 2020).

- The four studies improved the SEL of students in collaboration, problem solving, sound decision making, and effective communication (LER, 2021).

These findings and data points are encouraging for using PBL—especially with disadvantaged and underserved students. Furthermore, using the knowledge obtained in these resources (LER, 2021) can be very helpful in providing the theory and framework(s) that both individual and teaching teams will need to begin implementing and refining their use of PBL within their unique context.

That is how an initiative like PBL becomes sustainable in schools: taking what's been done—tweaking and adapting it—finally collecting data for informing and revising future practice. Don't let data collection throw you if it's a new concept. You can learn how to use data to guide your work by surveying participating teachers for confidence and self-efficacy for teaching using PBL. You can also monitor student engagement and achievement before and after exposure to PBL. Pre- and post-survey instruments are available on the companion website, resources.corwin.com/ProjectBasedLearning+. Feel free to revise and edit these surveys to meet the needs of your unique school context.

COMMON HURDLES TO IMPLEMENTING PBL

The previous section informs us that PBL works to improve learning—especially for underserved kids who may be struggling to keep up with their grade level. However, data is variable, and the same PBL treatment that works for one class may not work precisely the same for yours. That's because hurdles to success, kids' readiness to learn, and teacher understanding vary from place to place. PBL has been definitely shown to have a high influence on student engagement and achievement. But even with the research-informed framework(s) introduced and elaborated on in this book, we need to closely monitor how our students are experiencing our facilitation. Remember, teaching pedagogy is part science but it's also part art. The art is our personal style and how we facilitate and carry out our pedagogical strategies. I can't stress monitoring our own impact enough.

I've learned a lot from the thousands of teachers I've met through my coaching work, and many do not like it when professional development providers and authors do not acknowledge their pain points. Therefore, you'll find in this book that we will not avoid the elephant in the room when it comes to any item that may challenge the teacher confidence and self-efficacy needed for implementing any of the proposed strategies—beginning with PBL. Before diving into the elements of high-quality PBL, let's quickly dispel three of the biggest misconceptions and roadblocks to attempting PBL that I've heard from educators.

1. **I have to prepare my students for exams (or cover lots of content) and can't dedicate an entire school year or semester to planning or teaching this way.** I agree—do not abandon the teaching practice you have carefully honed. Instead, implement one project a semester, connect it to learning in your area as best as possible, and implement it for no more than two to three weeks at a time.

2. **I'm a content teacher and am not exactly sure how to make real-world projects.** I admit this can be tricky the first time around. Focus on important problems in the community (e.g., health, financial inclusion, environment). Let the students pick the issue(s) they want to tackle and develop a plan for knowing their topic inside and out, along with solutions. I curated resources for various topics of interest (see Figure 1.1) that you can use to help provide compelling inspiration to engage your kids.

FIGURE 1.1   PBL+ RESOURCES FOR SPECIAL
             INTERESTS AND PASSION PROJECTS

1. Art
2. Environmental
3. Financial Literacy
4. Health and Medical
5. Law
6. Music
7. Technology

For more details on these special interests, see https://bit.ly/3TbYoU2

3. **I typically teach my students the required content; after learning, they use
   their new knowledge to make a project. What do the teaching process and
   pacing look like in PBL, and how is it different from what I already do?**
   Think of the project you are teaching the same way you would a unit of
   study. Students engage and participate in projects (the unit)—not
   necessarily make them. More specifically, they learn throughout the project
   while developing and creating products (not projects) to transfer and
   showcase their learning. In coaching learners of all ages, I have found a
   greater impact on student learning when they complete their products in
   drafts and receive feedback using a straightforward protocol. This practice
   will be fully explained in Chapter 5.

   For now, let's examine the pacing chart in Figures 1.2 and 1.3 to
   understand better the progression of learning in projects along with pacing
   and teaching structure as students develop their products.

PACING AND TEACHING STRUCTURE IN PBL

FIGURE 1.2   ELEMENTARY SAMPLE PACING CHART FOR A TWO-WEEK
             PBL UNIT. THIS TEACHER SEES STUDENTS DAILY.

WEEK	MON	TUES	WED	THURS	FRI
One	Compelling Hook	Mini-Lesson, Work Time, and Reflection	Feedback Protocol and Work Time	Quiz and Work Time	Mini-Lesson, Work Time, and Reflection
Two	Feedback Protocol and Work Time	Mini-Lesson, Work Time, and Reflection	Discuss Draft With Teacher	Final Work Time and Reflection	Public Product and Reflection

WEEK	MON	TUES	WED	THURS	FRI
One	Compelling Hook and Guest Expert Speaker		Mini-Lesson, Work Time, and Reflection		Feedback Protocol and Work Time
Two		Mini-Lesson, Work Time, and Reflection		Feedback Protocol and Work Time	
Three	Discuss Draft With Teacher		Final Work Time and Reflection		Public Product and Reflection

In PBL, we launch projects with an exciting, compelling hook to inform students about the purpose of the unit and the products they'll be creating. We will learn more about creating compelling hooks in Chapter 9 on page 107. A good practice is to invite experts as guest speakers to make projects more compelling and authentic. But of course, this practice isn't only limited to the launch of projects. After the compelling hook, I like to manage lessons, activities, and learning in the following four-step process within a workshop model–inspired structure:

1. Mini-lesson (10–15 minutes)

2. Work time and reflection (35 minutes)

3. Feedback protocol (10–15 minutes)

4. More work time for either revision or continuing to the next draft and reflection (35 minutes).

   These timings are for two class periods at 50 minutes each. Adjust time frames depending on the length of your teaching block.

The four teaching steps and teaching structure are not perfect, but it's a structure I've used successfully to keep learning organized and evaluate students' work as they use feedback to revise their drafts systematically. I suggest skimping a bit on lengthy whole-group lessons and choosing to work with smaller groups during periods of ample work time to model, remediate gaps in previous learning, and reteach vital concepts as needed.

A SIMPLE, EFFECTIVE FRAMEWORK FOR PBL

The previous sections in this chapter provided us with the supporting research for PBL and the pacing and teaching structure we can use for facilitating projects. Still, teachers trying their hand at PBL may be uncertain as to how to strengthen their project ideas and make them the best possible learning experiences for students. A research-informed framework for PBL and a few strategies for defining and organizing the student experience can considerably improve outcomes. When executed effectively, the HQPBL framework provides elements like authenticity, project management, and public products for educators to create the conditions for learning to stick and continue after projects (Valenzuela, 2022a).

For example, content or elective teachers can increase authenticity in projects by bringing in industry experts (e.g., engineers, environmental scientists, computer programmers, activists) at the launch to introduce the type of work students will be learning to do (Adams-Stafford, 2019). Teachers can also help students improve their work by having them develop public products with a call to action advocating for causes they care about, and instructing audiences of community members on the next steps to take (Valenzuela, 2021d). Before diving further into the framework, let's quickly learn about its development.

Established in 2018, the HQPBL framework is the consensus of the research and the accumulated practice of PBL leaders and experts worldwide (see Figure 1.4). The work to devise the framework was led by the Buck Institute for Education (now PBLWorks) in partnership with the Project Management Institute Educational Foundation (PMIEF) and the William and Flora Hewlett Foundation. The process was guided by a 27-member steering committee and supported by a 90-member advisory team (Mergendoller, 2018). Other essential partners included Google, High Tech High, EL Education, Southern Regional Education Board, and the International Society for Technology Education (ISTE). An important project's goal was to provide teachers and schools with no access to formal PBL training with resources that enable them to enact PBL practices independently by having research-informed guidelines at their disposal for designing the student experience.

FIGURE 1.4   HQPBL FRAMEWORK

1. Intellectual challenge and accomplishment
2. Authenticity
3. Public product
4. Collaboration
5. Project management
6. Refection

SOURCE: hqpbl.org.

The HQPBL framework can be used with learners of all ages, but it's particularly well suited to middle and high school students who are passionate about solving meaningful problems. Furthermore, the framework advises that for PBL to be "high quality," six minimal criteria must be present throughout projects (see the following section).

USING THE HIGH-QUALITY PBL FRAMEWORK

My time in my PhD program taught me that knowledge is created through action research, which is why it's integral to my coaching work and also my own learning. Whenever you're studying something new, it's essential to explore what's already been done on that particular topic. Chances are someone has already developed a framework, model, or system we can learn from by adapting and tweaking it for our specific academic context. Therefore, "framework first, mindset second" is a powerful principle I use to help colleagues understand that having good general guidelines for doing something new is the prerequisite to developing second-nature expertise. Learning to design and implement projects is no different. The HQPBL framework can be an excellent place to start using PBL as a research-informed instructional approach.

This book doesn't jump straight into designing projects because we need to know the elements of a high-quality project before attempting to develop one. In my coaching work, I meet many educators who need just a little assistance in understanding what elements should be present in the projects they facilitate with students. I find that most are set to begin their PBL journey with a bit of guidance using a tool like the HQPBL framework. The framework helps educators define the student PBL experience and can be an authentic starting point for designing and implementing projects for any educator. Furthermore, we can use the following six elements from the HQPBL framework to frame what students should be doing, learning, and experiencing (Valenzuela, 2022a).

1. **Intellectual challenge and accomplishment.** Students investigate challenging problems or issues over an extended period of time. To keep the process and student learning manageable, I recommend two to three weeks for teachers new to PBL (see Figures 1.2 and 1.3). Two to three weeks is enough time for kids to develop a couple of solid products—one written and one they construct, design, or create (see #3 for the public product). Throughout the project, they should develop the essential content knowledge and concepts central to academic disciplines. Therefore, I encourage teachers to have students use the thinking routines and problem-solving strategies they typically use (e.g., Bloom's taxonomy, design thinking, scientific inquiry, computational thinking) to think critically in their content area.

2. **Authenticity.** Projects focus on real-world connections that are meaningful to students—including their cultures and backgrounds (Seidel, 2014). Framing a compelling project context for students is critical to having them care and get their buy-in about doing the work. Additionally, the tools and techniques they employ should mimic those used by career professionals. By inviting experts (Wolpert-Gawron, 2019) into the classroom and having students assume authentic career roles (e.g., engineer, doctor, auto technician), they can learn valuable career pathway options and see how their work and the solutions they develop impact others.

3. **Public product.** The students' final products are presented to the public as a culminating event. This means the work they produce is seen and discussed with the broader community, including parents, industry professionals, other classes, administrators, and community members. When students know that others will see their work, this may motivate them to put their best foot forward. Public products are not limited to

presentation nights. Student work can be displayed as public art, as exhibits, or online via social media, YouTube, and safe school websites.

Additionally, products can also be assessed as performance tasks. A performance task is a learning activity or assessment that students perform to transfer their knowledge, understanding, and skillsets. Performance tasks produce a tangible product or performance that is evidence of learning. I created this nifty table categorizing different products and performance tasks into five types (see Table 1.1).

TABLE 1.1 EXAMPLES OF PRODUCT AND PERFORMANCE TASK TYPES

DESIGNED AND DEVELOPED	TECHNOLOGICAL	MAPPING AND PLANNING	PRESENTATION AND DEMONSTRATION	COMPOSED
Art Gallery Exhibit	Animation	Blueprint	Debate	Analysis
Garden	App	Building Floorplan	Lesson Facilitation	Article
Machine	Computer Program	Business Plan	Mock Trial	Blog
Mode of Transportation (air, land, and water)	Digital Story/Comic	Business Proposal	Newscast	Brochure
Prototype	Infographic	Competitive Bid	Oral Defense	Call to Action
Scale Model	Invention	Computer Program Flow Chart	Panel Discussion	Design Journal
Structure (tower, bridge, etc.)	Photo Album	Customer Estimate	Performing Arts (acting, singing, and dancing)	Field Guide
Tiny House	Podcast	Design Sketch	Pitch	Letter
Woodwork (benches, chairs, shelves, etc.)	Robot	Project Management Plan	Public Demonstration	News Editorial
Working Model	Simulation	Project Timeline or Timetable	Public Service Announcement	Product Review
	Social Media Campaign		Speech	Research Report
	Video		Spoken Word	Scientific Journal
	Virtual Museum			Script
				Training Manual

online resources ⌐ Available for download at resources.corwin.com/ProjectBasedLearning+

4. **Collaboration.** Working with others is a PBL hallmark where students collaborate with adults and their peers in many different ways. Adults serve as mentors and guides and can include teachers, community members, or outside experts. In teamwork between students (Valenzuela, 2019a), each learner contributes their unique skills and talents to add to the whole group. Author Simon Sinek (2012) once tweeted, "A team is not a group of people who work together. A team is a group of people who trust each other." Learners of all ages need good collaboration tools to establish and maintain trust. Creating shared agreements, team contracts, and task lists is an excellent start. You can see these resources and more on the companion website, resources.corwin.com/ProjectBasedLearning+.

> *To weave literacy throughout projects for all learners, I recommend having students create two products per project: (1) something they make, and (2) something they write.*

5. **Project management.** Students help manage the project process, using tools and strategies similar to those used by adults. I've seen teachers using several tools for assisting learners in keeping their work organized—good ones for PBL include

   - scrum boards (LaVogue, 2020),
   - using design thinking during the ideation process (Rochester, 2019), and
   - maintaining important documents in a learning management system (e.g., Google Classroom or Schoology).

   I've also found that some learners benefit greatly from keeping a daily schedule before attempting to help manage projects. As students' capacity for self-management increases, teachers take on the role of facilitator, helping guide students through the process rather than directing it.

6. **Reflection.** The learning process is enhanced by frequent reflections that help students think about their progress and how to improve their work. To hit this point home, I share this quote from John Dewey (1933, p. 78) with teachers: "We do not learn from experience. We learn from reflecting on experience." To bring Dewey's quote to fruition, we can have learners complete products in drafts and jump-start reflection through critique protocols (Edutopia, 2016). This type of process can help learners retain content and skills longer and gives them the awareness of how they learn best by using reflection for metacognition. Other methods for reflection can include journaling, the 3-2-1 strategy (Garmston & Wellman, 2009), and the one-minute paper (Center for Excellence in Teaching and Learning, n.d.).

SUMMARY

For teachers new to PBL, doing projects can seem daunting, overwhelming, and perhaps outright tricky. Whether you teach in person, remotely, or in a hybrid model, PBL can be an important teaching strategy for producing high influences on student engagement and achievement in your ever-evolving classroom. I hope you consider the elements of HQPBL along with the pacing and teaching strategies proposed in this chapter. You will find these resources helpful whether you're beginning or enhancing your teaching using PBL. It just takes practice and patience to build your expertise and know-how. Now that you better understand what high-quality and research-informed PBL is, we will move into *Understanding the CASEL 5 and Emotional Intelligence*, the second element of the PBL+ Framework.

....

CHAPTER 2

ELEMENT 2: UNDERSTAND THE BASICS OF THE CASEL 5 (FOR SEL) AND EMOTIONAL INTELLIGENCE

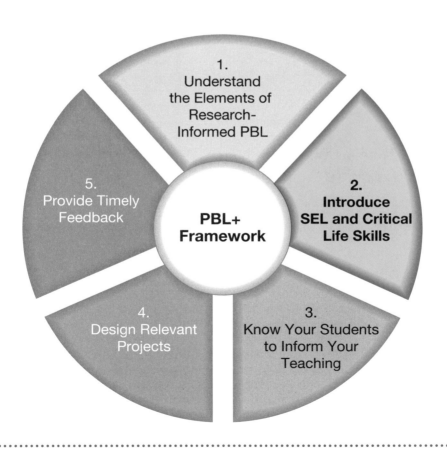

This chapter provides the foundational knowledge required for integrating social and emotional learning (SEL) into your project-based learning (PBL) units and the emotional intelligence (EQ) skills needed to successfully implement the subsequent steps in the PBL+ Framework. As you read this, you may wonder why I included SEL and EQ in a book for PBL+ or why they are included in a new PBL framework. The answer is simple: our kids have always struggled with their social and emotional well-being. Unfortunately, the pandemic has exacerbated the need for SEL—schools will need to help young people recover from emotional and mental health challenges experienced during COVID-19 (Centers for Disease Control and Prevention [CDC], 2021) and in life as they get older. To assist us, we will explore data reported by the CDC (2021) and learn strategies to increase our understanding of how to use SEL effectively in PBL.

PBL is not the only teaching methodology we can use to uplift SEL in classrooms, but high-quality PBL has been shown to effectively promote the SEL of students (Baines et al., 2021) and be a powerful addition to our teaching arsenal if we understand what we're trying to accomplish with students. Through my own action research, I have found that putting numbers to issues or topics we're studying can strengthen buy-in from colleagues and inform effective school programs. The goal here is to do such transformative and compelling work that others will want to join you and create similar learning experiences for their students. Furthermore, applying the knowledge in this chapter will help you activate SEL purposefully and as needed in both your non-PBL lessons and personal life.

LEARNING INTENTIONS

▶ Readers will be able to

- establish the need for uplifting SEL in PBL,
- review research that supports SEL across the curriculum,
- understand the multifaceted skillsets associated with the CASEL 5, and
- assist students with emotional regulation by implementing a tool designed to boost self- and social awareness.

STUDENTS NEED EMOTIONAL SUPPORT MORE THAN EVER

I remember my first year of teaching as being difficult, and then each subsequent year it got easier as I improved at the job. However, the last three school years have been the most difficult I've had to navigate as both a student and a 20-year veteran teacher. For many educators, each of the last three years has also become more challenging to navigate, and the emotional toll on students is devastating. The Centers for Disease Control and Prevention (CDC) reported their first representative survey on the mental health of high school students in the U.S. during the COVID-19 pandemic. In 2021 the data revealed that our children are hurting and tell us the following (CDC, 2021):

- 37% of high school students reported they experienced poor mental health during the COVID-19 pandemic.

- 44% said they persistently felt sad or hopeless during the time in quarantine in 2020.

- 36% of students reported experiencing racism before or during the COVID-19 pandemic. The highest among Asian students at 64% and 55% of Black students and students of multiple races.

Things haven't been easy for some students in family life either. The report (CDC, 2021) also revealed the following:

- 55% reported enduring emotional abuse by a parent or caregiver, including swears, insults, and put-downs.

- 11% experienced physical abuse by a parent or caregiver, including various forms of physical violence.

- 29% reported that a parent or caregiver lost a job.

It's clear from the data that many American youths are living through tremendous trauma and feel they cannot rely on the most important adults in their lives. Many are sitting in classrooms attempting to learn through their trauma. If it's overwhelming for us to teach them, imagine how they feel, and the social and emotional skills many will need to learn at school because they can't get them from home.

There is an undeniable need for us to integrate SEL into classroom learning— especially now that many school systems have begun opening back up post-pandemic. This is also an opportunity for educators to help students with the social and emotional support they actually need. Kathleen A. Ethier, PhD, director of CDC's Division of Adolescent and School Health, states:

> School connectedness is a key to addressing youth adversities at all times—especially during times of severe disruptions. . . . Students need our support now more than ever, whether by making sure that their schools are inclusive and safe or by providing opportunities to engage in their communities and be mentored by supportive adults. (CDC, 2021, para. 8)

Luckily the education world is no longer a stranger to SEL or its five competencies known as the CASEL 5—designed for teachers to integrate into their lessons by the Collaborative for Academic, Social, and Emotional Learning (CASEL, n.d.-b.). We will now dive into the basics of the CASEL 5 and later integrate them as the central skills in projects uplifting the core elements of effective projects in Part 2 of this book.

THE CASEL 5

CASEL is the leader in research and resources for understanding and implementing SEL (CASEL, n.d.-a). CASEL lists five SEL competencies educators can use to help learners better understand their environment, themselves, and others, known and referred to as the *CASEL 5* (CASEL, n.d.-b.). When enacted in lessons properly, the CASEL 5 can provide learners with the foundational EQ and life skills necessary to become better students and people. The CASEL 5 and associated skills include, but are not limited to, the following:

1. **Self-awareness:** The ability to correctly understand the impact of one's own emotions on their thoughts, body, and behavior. Self-awareness skills include the following:
   - Expressing one's emotions accurately by labeling them
   - Understanding how difficult emotions impact overall well-being
   - Taking an accurate personal inventory of one's strengths and limitations
   - Setting attainable goals
   - Possessing high levels of confidence and a positive mindset

2. **Self-management:** The ability to manage one's thoughts and behaviors and effectively work toward the attainment of personal, academic, or professional goals. Social-management strategies include the following:
   - Regulating emotions
   - Thinking critically to problem-solve in complex and high-stress situations
   - Controlling impulses
   - Delaying personal gratification for the greater good
   - Empowering one's self-motivation
   - Completing tasks (e.g., assignments, chores, responsibilities)

3. **Social awareness:** The ability to empathize and take the perspective of others (including diverse individuals), even when it doesn't align with one's own life outlook or values. Social awareness qualities include the following:
   - Empathizing with others
   - Recognizing and appreciating diversity
   - Knowing standards of appropriate behavior along with social and ethical norms
   - Having good listening skills

4. **Relationship skills:** The ability to foster healthy and uplifting personal and professional relationships, including with people from diverse backgrounds. Good relationship skills include the following:
   - Respecting others unconditionally
   - Communicating clearly and appropriately to the intended audience

- Listening to understand
- Collaborating well with others
- Resisting social pressure when it conflicts with one's values
- Resolving conflicts fairly
- Seeking assistance from others

5. **Responsible decision making:** The ability to make well-thought-out decisions while monitoring the impact on self and others and honoring ethical, safety, and social norms. Good decision making includes the following:
   - Being outcomes orientated
   - Monitoring one's intention and impact
   - Making inferences based on facts and evidence
   - Using critical thinking skills to analyze alternatives in the decision-making process
   - Considering one's well-being and that of others before deciding

Teachers beginning to implement the CASEL 5 into lessons should consider that all of the five competencies are related and can function concurrently. The three project exemplars in Part 2 of this book will feature their interconnectedness so that teachers can intentionally begin integrating SEL skillsets where they logically fit—instead of in isolation. For example, in CASEL's integrated framework graphic, *self-awareness* and *self-management* focus on skillsets related to self and are featured in the color orange. *Social awareness* and *relationship skills* concentrate on skills and attributes related to others and appear in the color green (CASEL, 2021). And *responsible decision-making skills* work simultaneously with the other four (CASEL, 2021).

Making students aware of these correlations throughout learning can also help them understand the multifaceted use of the SEL skills they're learning along with academic and career knowledge. Furthermore, teachers should emphasize how one competency works with the others with students (see Table 2.1, page 26). These are powerful emotional intelligence-building concepts for learners of all ages to understand, and ones that Part 2 of this book will further explore in Chapters 6–8.

For the emotional growth addressed in Table 2.1 to occur, students must frequently practice applying skills in the CASEL 5—repetition is the mother of skill. According to Hattie (2009), an important item for teachers to consider is that although modeling and discussing SEL strategies with students as needed is impactful to learning—interventions are most effective when applied in 40 lessons or more. Student growth, therefore, requires educators to intentionally and thoughtfully weave the CASEL 5 into their instruction. The following section provides grounding research to support applying the CASEL 5 SEL framework in classroom lessons and projects.

**TABLE 2.1   THE INTERCONNECTEDNESS OF THE CASEL 5
SEL COMPETENCIES**

CASEL 5 COMPETENCY	STUDENT LEARNING	CONNECTIONS TO ANOTHER COMPETENCY
Self-Awareness	Students learn about self-awareness by beginning to explore how they experience difficult emotions.	Students can now find and implement strategies for regulating difficult emotions to strengthen the self-management process.
Self-Management	Students learn that self-management involves critical thinking as well as impulse control.	Students can now learn to use responsible decision-making strategies by weighing the pros and cons of their actions and behavior.
Social Awareness	Students learn that empathy is critical to relationship building.	Students can now use relationship skills that uplift the importance of understanding and honoring the experience of others.
Relationship Skills	Students learn about how social pressure from peers may cause them to participate in bullying weaker peers.	Students can now learn to use responsible decision-making strategies by choosing to become an ally.
Responsible Decision Making	Students learn how their good decisions can positively impact them and others in their school community.	Students can now learn to use strategies that promote both social awareness and self-management skills.

RESEARCH THAT INFORMED THE CASEL SEL FRAMEWORK

Through years of rigorous research beginning in 1994, CASEL has developed the CASEL 5 integrated framework and has advanced the scientific base for SEL by continuously refining their own research, aligning efforts with notable work in the field, and spotlighting essential studies. Unfortunately, I haven't seen many school districts delve into the research or conduct their own to determine what works for them. Instead, they purchase SEL curriculum and expect teachers to implement it without personalizing the content for students. This approach usually won't work for every learner and may cause teachers to view SEL as one more item they need to check off their to-do list. Previous meta-analyses show that SEL is not a "one-size-fits-all" intervention. The highest impact (largest effect size) occurs when SEL experiences are intentionally personalized to learners' unique context or culture (Sklad et al., 2012; Taylor et al., 2017; Wiglesworth et al., 2016).

You shouldn't feel like you have to design SEL activities for your PBL units from scratch or think that scripted resources have no value. Instead, I encourage you to tweak, personalize, and adapt resources as you consider your students' unique SEL and academic needs. After all, element four of the PBL+ Framework invites you to adapt projects but make them your own. There's nothing wrong with drawing inspiration from reputable works as long as we are not sticking to a script. This chapter intentionally provides the foundational activities you can adapt to help both you and your kids begin strengthening EQ skills—having this insight will improve your ability to adapt confidently. Furthermore, in Part 2 of this book you will find three adaptable PBL units uplifting the CASEL 5 for you to make your own. I will suggest the sections you can personalize to impact learning best in your unique space. For now, let's continue exploring some of the supporting research.

Over 300 studies captured in four major meta-analyses support SEL in helping with academic and emotional development in both short- and long-term scenarios (Mahoney et al., 2018). A landmark meta-analysis combining data of 213 studies involving over 270,000 learners reveals that when SEL is a part of the core curriculum for multiple years, the impact on behavior and learning in schools is positive in the following ways (Durlak et al., 2011):

- Improved social behaviors and lower levels of distress
- Reduced aggression and emotional distress among students
- Increased *helping behaviors* in school
- Improved positive attitudes toward self and others
- Improved academic performance by program's end
- Increased age academic performance by 11 percent points

More encouraging data show that SEL can have long-term positive impacts on academics (up to 18 years) and personal life (such as emotional distress and substance use)—as shown in another meta-analysis involving 82 studies and 100,000 students from various countries (Taylor et al., 2017).

As you conclude this section and as we jump into the how-to, I want you to glean two essential items we learn from these data points.

1. SEL can help students live better overall lives.

2. SEL can be an academic intervention because it helps students better prepare for learning and has been shown to improve academic outcomes.

Now that we are better grounded in the critical life skills associated with the competencies in the CASEL 5 and have explored the supporting evidence for SEL, it might be easier to commit to weaving SEL into our everyday teaching. To make this pedagogical transformation smoother and to make a lasting impact on learners, consider the CASEL 5 and its set of skills as integral to student learning as the content standards uplifted in your daily lessons. If having to teach these numerous skills appears daunting—especially when you're responsible for getting through extensive content—focus on the grounding EQ skills first. I suggest beginning with your learner's unique relationship with their own emotions. They must learn to walk before learning to run.

DEMYSTIFY EMOTIONS FOR STUDENTS

Demystifying emotions for students is critical to helping them begin to understand and conquer their difficult ones and vital for assisting them in finding a peaceful state when the learning process is disrupted. Furthermore, assisting students in understanding how they uniquely experience emotions is foundational to helping them improve their EQ and other vital SEL skills (Valenzuela, 2020). Psychology tells us that emotion is a complicated state of feeling with the power to impact people's physical and psychological changes (Cherry, 2022). Our brain creates emotions by assigning meaning to bodily sensations from our lived experiences (Zimmerman, 2019). Furthermore, people experience emotions and feelings in sequential order—emotions precede feelings (Meyer, 2012), and feelings precede our moods and behavior (Valenzuela, 2021a). Unfortunately, many people (both young and old) are unaware of the depth of their emotions and how they differ from feelings, thus impacting every aspect of their life. We manifest emotions either consciously or subconsciously, bringing about feelings that we experience consciously. See Figure 2.1 for a simple illustration of the progression of emotions.

FIGURE 2.1 PROGRESSION OF EMOTIONS

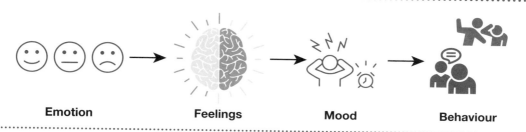

| Emotion | Feelings | Mood | Behaviour |

IMAGE SOURCES: iStock.com/Illerlok_Xolms, iStock.com/filo, iStock.com/matsabe, and iStock.com/appleuzr

online resources Available for download at resources.corwin.com/ProjectBasedLearning+

It's important to stress to learners that although every person experiences emotions, not every person experiences emotions in the same way. Therefore, understanding the relationship between one's lived experience is vital to deepening their understanding of how they experience emotions, especially the difficult ones. For example, fear is a powerful and primitive emotion that all humans experience, just like other emotions (anger, joy, surprise, etc.). Psychology research informs us that emotional fear involves both a universal biochemical response and a high individual emotional response alerting people to imminent danger or the threat of harm—whether physical or psychological (Fritscher, 2023). Some of us can regulate and overcome fear(s) easier than others—depending on personal trauma, exposure to good tools and resources, and ultimately heightened levels of EQ.

For example, I lived in poverty while growing up in Queens, New York. I experienced emotional fear, just like others in my peer group who did not experience poverty or grow up in Queens. Due to the difference in our life circumstances, I'm guessing some of the factors that cause them and me to experience fear and anxiety probably differ significantly. Although I can't prove my inference, it's still worth considering for assisting kids in understanding the correlations between their lived experiences and the power their emotions have on their mind, body, and behavior. Growing up, I feared not having enough food to eat, nice clothing to wear, and the unchecked physical and verbal bullying that often occurred in my neighborhood. I can't speak for others from different life circumstances, but their fear factors will most likely differ from mine. Moreover, having different life circumstances does not mean that the fear (or difficult emotions) someone experiences doesn't cause trauma or require them to learn how to regulate it effectively. After all, fear is very real to the person experiencing it.

As we know, fear isn't the only challenging emotion youth experience daily, including in the classroom. Unfortunately, many students haven't been exposed to SEL in the classroom and are unsure how to regulate their emotions. That's where teachers can help. Learners need to be able to take a metaphoric step back when overcome with complex emotions to reflect and redirect them using a repository of trusted tools and strategies they know when and how to use. These strategies can help heal from past emotional trauma and restore inner peace daily—even when addressing discouraging situations like difficult people or a setback. A simple tool to help regulate emotions can help provide the needed steps no matter what they encounter in their life. Also, the EQ skills they develop using a simple tool (see Figure 2.2) can provide the knowledge of self that's foundational for mastering other SEL-related skills.

USE AN EMOTIONAL INTELLIGENCE PLANNER

In an episode of *Queen Sugar* (one of my favorite shows), a main character, Micah West, said, "I can't control what happens, but I can control how to respond to things." This is an empowering outlook, even in the most dispiriting times. To help kids improve their responses when faced with difficult emotions, I developed a handy three-step Emotional Intelligence Planner (Valenzuela, 2021a) by using my insights from two trusted sources and listening to participant feedback in action research (Valenzuela, 2022e). These are the two sources that mainly inspired the Emotional Intelligence Planner:

1. The processing model of emotion regulation was developed by Stanford professor James Gross (1998, 2015). His research concludes that people can learn to modulate and alter the emotions they experience (Gross, 2015).

2. Plutchik's (2001) wheel of emotions, which helps learners accurately identify the emotions they experience in different situations to determine their emotional triggers. The wheel simplifies emotions by focusing on eight primary ones: (1) anger, (2) anticipation, (3) joy, (4) trust, (5) fear, (6) surprise, (7) sadness, and (8) disgust.

To get kids to begin labeling their emotions accurately, use Plutchik's wheel of emotions to recognize their emotions in different situations. Don't only have them focus on negative situations. I like to also have them investigate the emotions they experience when they have a moment of success, explore a natural setting, or do something they enjoy. This crucial practice categorizes emotions and responses to them, allowing them to learn more about their emotional states. Additionally, with practice using Plutchik's wheel, students can begin recognizing that other emotions they experience uniquely are an amalgam of the eight basic emotions and may also intersect with secondary ones (Plutchik, 2001). People also experience secondary emotions, which are emotional reactions to an emotion, such as the feeling of shame when afraid or feeling joy resulting from happiness.

Plutchik's wheel of emotions has been simplified for children ages 4–11 using emojis to represent 10 emotions with no subcategories (Mentally Healthy Schools, n.d.).

Once kids are familiar with naming emotions, they can begin to identify emotional triggers. This practice is critical for them to plan responses with good self-regulation tactics and understand the unique impact of their emotions on their overall well-being and social interactions. To purposefully assist them with gauging where their emotions reside and identify strategies for regulating them effectively, use the Emotional Intelligence Planner (see Figure 2.2). This simple check-in can be in response to feeling off or having trouble restoring their inner peace after a difficult social interaction or an intense moment with a peer or caregiver. Sometimes youth will resist leaning into a problematic emotion. In that case, please don't rush the process; allow them space and time to restore inner peace. Once the intensity of the emotion has subsided, warmly encourage them to complete the planner and advise them that difficult emotions are vital to informing us where we need to focus and improve.

FIGURE 2.2 VALENZUELA'S EMOTIONAL INTELLIGENCE PLANNER

TRIGGERING SITUATION	LABEL EMOTIONS	SEL STRATEGY
Use the space provided to describe the situation that triggered you emotionally.	Eight primary emotions: ☐ Anger ☐ Anticipation ☐ Joy ☐ Trust ☐ Fear ☐ Surprise ☐ Sadness ☐ Disgust Use the space provided to elaborate on secondary emotions you may be experiencing. Use Plutchik's (2001) wheel of emotions as a reference.	☐ Self-management ☐ Social awareness ☐ Relationship skills ☐ Self-awareness ☐ Responsible decision making Use the space provided to elaborate on how you will use the EQ skills to regulate your emotions and find solutions to the problem.

online resources 🔖 Available for download at resources.corwin.com/ProjectBasedLearning+

Not every learner will initially find the EQ planner easy to complete. Remind students that emotions and feelings don't always last long (Cavell, 2004), but they will reappear when they are triggered. It's therefore critical to get a handle on understanding how their emotions impact them. Consider the EQ planner activity a cognitive process that students can use during projects and throughout the day to label and regulate emotions, restore their inner peace, and prepare for learning. Inform students that the planner is a helpful tool to help them organize their thoughts, new knowledge, reflections, and next steps regarding their complex emotions.

Furthermore, showing them a completed planner example (Figure 2.3) can help them know that other students (and adults) face difficult emotions and also need assistance managing them. I get better responses from students when they know they're not the only ones using or needing the tool.

FIGURE 2.3 VALENZUELA'S COMPLETED EMOTIONAL INTELLIGENCE PLANNER

TRIGGERING SITUATION	LABEL EMOTIONS	SEL STRATEGIES
My teacher partnered me to work with James on the class project. Working with him is fun because he is my friend, and I like being around him. The problem is he does not complete his portion of the work on time and does not listen to me when I remind him about it. For us to get a good grade, I also began to do his work. I do not want to tell my teacher because I feel James will stop being my friend.	Eight primary emotions: ☒ Anger ☐ Anticipation ☐ Joy ☐ Trust ☐ Fear ☐ Surprise ☐ Sadness ☒ Disgust Use the space provided to elaborate on secondary emotions you may be experiencing. Use Plutchik's (2001) wheel of emotions as a reference: **I feel annoyance.**	☐ Self-management ☒ Social awareness ☒ Relationship skills ☒ Self-awareness ☐ Responsible decision making Use the space provided to elaborate on how you will use the EQ skills to regulate your emotions and find solutions to the problem: **Self-awareness:** I labeled the emotion(s) I experienced. **Social awareness:** To empathize with James, I speak with him to learn what causes him not to complete his work. **Relationship skills:** I will need to set my boundaries firmly and respectfully and seek assistance from our teacher if he doesn't do his own work.

TIPS FOR USING THE EMOTIONAL INTELLIGENCE PLANNER

Coaching students through self and social awareness using tools like the EQ planner can assist them with managing their emotions. A tool like this can also help them accept themselves and others, understand their situations, and be less self-judgmental when experiencing unpleasant feelings like jealousy, anger, or annoyance. Before moving to the next chapter, I want to offer a few tidbits for you to consider for having learners get the most effective use of the EQ planner.

- Encourage learners to state the triggering situation objectively by sticking to the facts of what actually happened. Don't add to or take away from the event (column one).

- Have them label their emotions without negatively judging themselves or others (column two).

- Remind them this activity is not meant to change the behavior of others. Instead, they should focus on improving their responses to the triggering situation (column three).

- Improved EQ will take time and repetition. According to Hattie (2009), for SEL strategies to be highly impactful to student learning, interventions should be applied in 40 lessons or more.

- SEL does not replace professional trauma-informed therapy, nor should SEL skills be taught or utilized independently of the curriculum (Cohen et al., 2021).

SUMMARY

Understanding the basics of the CASEL 5 and EQ provides helpful foundational knowledge to begin activating SEL across your lessons and PBL units. Our students need SEL more than ever. The research-based resources in this chapter help teachers consider the implementation of SEL competencies to serve their unique community of learners best. Additionally, the Emotional Intelligence Planner is a simple tool designed to get learners started on their journey to emotional regulation by taking the time to unpack and regulate their difficult and triggering emotions. We now segue into Chapter 3, and the third element of the PBL+ Framework: *Use Knowledge of Students to Inform Teaching*. We will learn to use what we know about our students to get to know them as people and learners and make sound instructional decisions.

CHAPTER 3

ELEMENT 3: USE KNOWLEDGE OF STUDENTS TO INFORM TEACHING

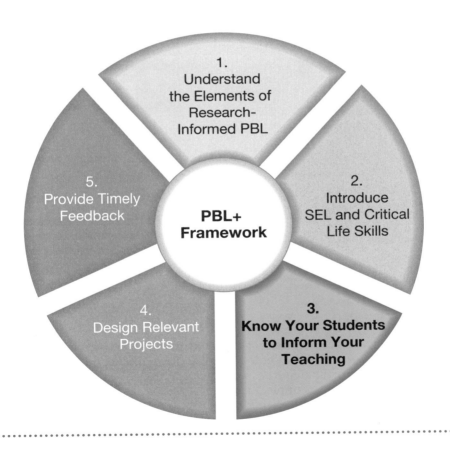

1.
Understand the Elements of Research-Informed PBL

2.
Introduce SEL and Critical Life Skills

**3.
Know Your Students to Inform Your Teaching**

4.
Design Relevant Projects

5.
Provide Timely Feedback

**PBL+
Framework**

In Chapter 1, we established that the elements of research-informed project-based learning (PBL) help teachers define the student experience. Chapter 2 focused on what we want to teach in regard to social and emotional learning (SEL) within the PBL structure. This element of the PBL+ Framework helps us prioritize our teaching using a research-informed PBL structure. The strategies in this chapter will help you curate the appropriate knowledge about your students so that you can use what you glean and know about them to personalize and tailor your SEL-infused PBL units to meet their learning needs better. Using knowledge of students is critical so that lessons in projects do not become one-size-fits-all and thus only benefit the learners who are more supported and prepared for the rigors of school.

To use our knowledge of students for the most impact requires us to get to know them as both individuals (people) and learners. This chapter provides a simple, but very powerful, tool for using what we know about our learners to teach and design lessons that don't skimp on instructional rigor. Both individual PBL teachers and teaching teams can sequentially implement these elements from the PBL+ Framework as a formula to impact student engagement and academic achievement in content, career, and SEL. These prescribed elements can also improve outcomes for underserved learners and create the intellectually safe spaces youth need to thrive—right in your classroom.

LEARNING INTENTIONS

► Readers will be able to

- establish the need for using what we know about students to establish relationships and making informed instructional decisions,

- review research that supports knowing students as people and learners, and

- understand the empathy mapping process.

WHY TEACHERS NEED TO KNOW STUDENTS' INTERESTS, SKILLS, AND LEARNING NEEDS

In this context, using our knowledge of students has two significant items for teachers to consider—we must get to know them as both individuals and learners (Hinton, 2021). Unfortunately, the importance of this isn't always crystalized for beginning teachers. For example, in my preservice learning program, I learned general knowledge about the science of early childhood development and lesson design but very little about getting to know youth as people. As a result, each student in my classes did not benefit from my early two years of instruction. Eventually I discovered that for the lessons in my PBL units to be compelling and practical, I would need to tailor them in fun and creative ways to engage every learner to the best of my ability. I also realized that getting to know them was the first step in this pedagogical transformation—requiring a reliable system for uncovering their unique interests, skills, and learning needs.

To make this point clearer, here are two important items to consider. Teachers who don't know their students well cannot design personalized student-centered learning and motivational experiences to help them thrive socially and academically (Barkley, 2019). On the other hand, teachers who know their students as both people and learners are familiar with their strengths, interests, and social-emotional needs and can thus help them thrive socially and academically (Schultz, 2015). Therefore, as instructional designers and PBL teachers or coaches, we must take on the task of knowing our students as individuals to discern the best way to teach them academic content.

But how do we know our learners as people? We can begin by paying attention to their areas of interest, their strengths, and the critical aspects of their cultural background. Culture comprises several factors that contribute to a student's identity and what they care about, including their familial customs and traditions, religion, language spoken at home, the music they listen to, and sports they like or participate in (National Geographic, n.d.). Knowing these aspects of kids helps us better understand what truly matters to them most—their personal and social needs, motivations, and overall personalities. Moreover, understanding them as individuals can be leveraged to connect with them through rapport and positive relationships—a vital prerequisite to forming learning partnerships (Valenzuela, 2022e). When what we know about them as people is meshed with what we know about them as learners, we better position ourselves to use our knowledge of students to co-create with them the learning experiences they need to become better people and students.

EMPATHY MAPPING FOR GETTING TO KNOW STUDENTS

Many of the teachers I meet in my PBL sessions feel that they know their students as learners and can explain how they learn best as well as their critical knowledge gaps. However, many are unsure about their interests, goals, and cultural assets beyond what they see at school. Important cultural assets to students may include a deep appreciation of and connection to the arts, music, language, traditions, and histories of their community's identity and customs, such as religious ceremonies and holidays (Groundwork USA, n.d.). When teachers have large classes, many also say it's impossible to get to know every student. I agree. We can only do our best by leading with empathy and beginning to learn more about those students who need us the most using a simple tool called an empathy map.

Empathizing with learners is a critical first step for getting to know them and making sound instructional decisions. Researchers who study emotions define empathy as the ability to sense other people's emotions in tandem with imagining what they might think or feel (Greater Good Magazine, n.d.). To jumpstart the process, there are several ways of getting to know students throughout the instructional day. For example, teachers can learn about them in classroom discussions, pay attention to what they care about (social issues, cultural norms, etc.), and recognize their gifts and abilities in transferring learning and in things they voluntarily discuss. Empathy maps can be a great way to organize the pertinent knowledge of students you gleaned about the kid(s) you're getting to know.

Empathy mapping was first conceived by Dave Gray, founder of XPLANE, in user experience design for understanding audiences (May, 2021). Popularized in the business world, empathy maps are a tool many companies use in product development to visually capture knowledge about their customers' experience with their products (D. Gray et al., 2010). Common labels on empathy maps used by businesses include *thoughts* and *feelings* and *think and feel*, and *say* and *do* after trying a product. For the purposes of getting to know students and curriculum planning, I have made a few modifications to empathy map labels, which will be explained further following Figure 3.1.

FIGURE 3.1 EMPATHY MAP TEMPLATE

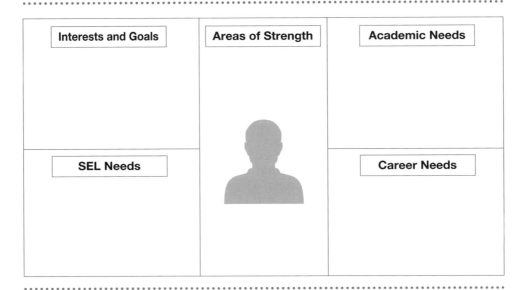

IMAGE SOURCE: iStock.com/kowalska-art

online resources Available for download at resources.corwin.com/ProjectBasedLearning+

THE BENEFITS OF EMPATHY MAPS

The benefits of empathy mapping extend beyond design and business too. In education, empathy maps are also used by countless educators to connect with students by empathizing and better understanding their behaviors, attitudes, academic needs, areas of strength, personal struggles, emotional states, and other attributes (Peixoto & Moura, 2020). Empathy mapping is also used to assist grade-level planning teams in purposefully empathizing with their students and developing more personalized learning experiences for them (Bland, 2020). In my PBL workshops, teaching teams work backward using empathy mapping, followed by personalizing curriculum and lesson design and alignment. Empathy maps also have benefits that extend beyond PBL (Valenzuela, 2021e, 2021c). They provide the following:

- Pertinent student information in one visual reference

- A better understanding of students and their life/academic circumstances

- An equity-based, collaborative tool for teachers and other stakeholders who interact with the same students, which can be helpful for students struggling academically or those who are socially isolated

- Consideration for SEL content to uplift in lessons
- Additional opportunities to make better instructional decisions based on the actual needs of students
- Callouts of key insights gleaned from data or research
- A synthesis of research observations and more in-depth insights about students' academic needs

The exercise of empathy mapping can also help teachers become more culturally and socially competent by frequently improving their knowledge of students. This authentic knowledge allows them to deliver more relevant projects and approach interactions and instruction from learners' point of view before creating their lessons. Therefore, I recommend mapping early during the project ideation stages to determine what learning outcomes would be equitable for students. You may also use your maps to provide a project theme or learning context. For example, if your learners are passionate about a particular cause (deforestation, recycling, etc.) or social issue (poverty, fair housing, civil rights, etc.), allow them to explore the topic and find solutions for their project.

GATHER DATA FOR YOUR EMPATHY MAP

Constructing empathy maps is a straightforward process once you gather pertinent information about your students—this is what knowledge of students means. The information we collect should include their personal goals, hobbies, interests, and areas of academic, career, and SEL needs, as well as data from assessments (e.g., benchmarks and formal formative assessments). The map we develop captures what we need to know in one visual snapshot, which we can later use to make sound instructional decisions. To construct your empathy map, you may use polls and surveys to inform you about their goals and interests. Use student work (e.g., reflection journals, essays, portfolios, and assessment data) to inform you of their learning needs accurately. We can also glean knowledge about our students in daily classroom discussions, paying attention to what they care about, recognizing their unique talents, and in things they voluntarily discuss. Use the labels in Figure 3.1 and the video I created (Valenzuela, 2021c) to simplify this process for you.

Also, be mindful that sometimes your learners will change throughout the school year. So should your perspective when empathizing with them. I encourage you to update your empathy maps as needed throughout the school year (each semester, every couple of months, etc.). The key here is to use what we know to create a better school experience for them. Some examples of using what we know about students through our curations may include developing unit or project themes they care about, considering how they may want to transfer learning through the products they create, and the themes of other class-based activities (field trips, clubs, etc.).

Additionally, teachers often ask me if they should complete a map for every student in their classes. Given that many teachers teach well over 100 students a semester or school year, I don't think that's possible. Instead, I recommend beginning with the student(s) that needs you the most. Students who need you the most need equity raised for them—and may include at-risk youth and kids who feel isolated from other classmates. Consulting with specialists at the school, such as the school counselor, to complete your maps is also an excellent way to learn how to raise equity for needy learners.

CONSTRUCTING AN EMPATHY MAP

Once you have gathered some pertinent data, you can begin mapping. Please treat this as a fun and informative activity, resulting in a valuable artifact to increase your understanding of how to help students academically and socially. It won't always be perfect, but it's a start toward creating a more equitable classroom for vulnerable students. I highly recommend grade-level teaching teams working together to complete maps for students they share. The only materials needed are chart paper, sticky notes, and markers. You may also print the empathy map template for your use with the following five sections:

1. **Interests and goals.** Items of interest to a learner motivate, inspire, and emotionally compel them to pursue them.

2. **Areas of strength.** These are areas in which a student excels and shines. Knowing their assets can be leveraged by using what they are good at to help them build on areas of improvement.

3. **Academic needs.** Areas of academic weakness in this section of the empathy map will vary among the content areas (i.e., English language arts, math, science, and social studies). Pay close attention to important concepts and skills that they will need for making cross-curricular connections. Here are some examples of concepts and skills that cut across multiple disciplines:
   - Ability to interpret informational text
   - Understanding cause and effect
   - Unit conversion (proportional reasoning)
   - Developing habits of mind
   - Using design thinking for designing from the perspective of the end user
   - Disaggregated summative and formative assessment of key data points can also be addressed here for helping to drive future remedial/instruction focuses.

4. **SEL needs.** The integrated framework developed by the Collaborative for Academic, Social, and Emotional Learning (CASEL) offers essential competence areas that students need to hone their understanding, abilities, and attitudes across. These include self-awareness, self-management, social awareness, relationship skills, and responsible decision making.

5. **Career needs.** Career needs are optional in empathy mapping, as not all teachers focus their instruction on careers. However, content-area teachers should make career connections to the academic concepts and skills they teach. Essential career skills like self-management, problem-solving, and the four Cs (communication, collaboration, creativity, and critical thinking) can also be addressed as needed. Career and technical education (CTE) teachers should identify areas of weakness that prevent learners from being fully informed about the essential items to consider when developing or following an individual college and career plan.

To strengthen your PBL lessons and units, you are not bound to use only the five labels suggested on the previous page (see Figures 3.1 and 3.2). Instead, you may personalize the process and include labels relevant to your teaching context. The most important result of completing this activity is connecting with students and making better-informed instructional decisions.

FIGURE 3.2   COMPLETED EMPATHY MAP EXAMPLE FOR AN ENGLISH LANGUAGE LEARNER

Interests and Goals	Areas of Strength	Academic Needs
• Improve English speaking and writing skills • Become an engineer • Loves to play fútbol (soccer) and Latin dance	• Fluent in Spanish • Empathetic toward others • Good listener	• Improve decoding skills in reading • Exposure to academic language • Learn more about how engineering design works
SEL Needs • Labeling emotions • Managing stress • Asking for help	 • Systems thinker • Mastered multiple Latin dances	**Career Needs** • Initiative • Project management • Being punctual • Flexibility and adaptability

IMAGE SOURCE: iStock.com/kowalska-art

SUMMARY

If your teaching experience is anything like mine, I'm guessing you, too, must dedicate some time to figuring out how to engage best to compel your unique students so that they can achieve academically and socially. This requires getting to know them as people and establishing rapport so we can make informed instructional decisions. I encourage you to use the empathy map template in this chapter to capture these important details about your students. In the coming chapters, we will use the knowledge we glean about students to frame our SEL-infused projects in ways that reflect them, their cultures, and their backgrounds. Now that we know the right things about our kids, we have the know-how for the next element of the PBL+ Framework, *Design Projects Relevant to the Students You Serve*.

CHAPTER 4

....

ELEMENT 4: DESIGN PROJECTS RELEVANT TO THE STUDENTS YOU SERVE

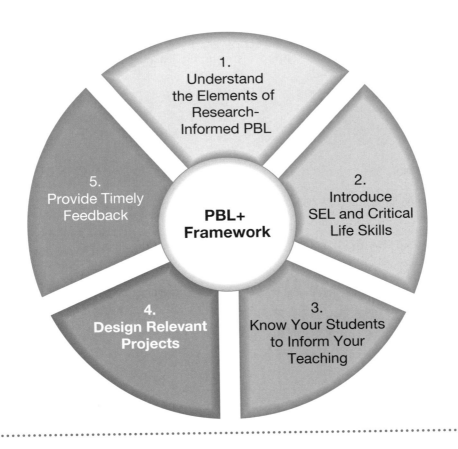

The previous elements in the PBL+ Framework were designed to help you learn the subject matter (project-based learning [PBL] and social and emotional learning [SEL]) and your students by working backward. In this element, you'll be able to take everything you know about PBL, SEL, your teaching content, and your students to confidently design and facilitate a relevant project unit for your unique student population. Confidence is essential to your teaching PBL well—so we will address that too. To help you plan projects, I will provide some essentials of sound core instruction and introduce you to the versatile Project and Performance Task Planner I created for my workshops. This planner is ideal for teachers wishing to facilitate full-blown PBL units or a shorter performance task—what I like to call a mini project. I will model the planner's use in Part 2 of this book for organizing the learning of three SEL-infused projects. The planner is also versatile enough to be utilized for daily lessons.

Some teachers I coach like to have their students complete only one performance task because the experience allows them to showcase real-world skills. Another vital component of the Project and Performance Task Planner is the attention to core instruction. As an instructional coach, I often work with school and district leaders who want help to shore up their teaching staff's ability to deliver effective core instruction, also known as Tier 1 instruction (Bowen, 2021). As you'll learn in the following pages of this chapter, core instruction should also be weaved into PBL. Solid core instruction is a good backdrop for the differentiation strategies required to support struggling learners and kids with diverse needs (Valenzuela, 2022i).

LEARNING INTENTIONS

▶ Readers will be able to

- establish the need for learning the building blocks of effective core instruction for becoming a confident teacher,

- understand the components of core instruction and how they can be used in PBL.

- familiarize yourself with the Project and Performance Task Planner, and

- review the sections of the planner to gain insights into sound teaching practices for planning and facilitating projects.

BECOME A CONFIDENT PBL TEACHER BY FOCUSING ON CORE INSTRUCTION

In my PBL coaching work, I'm big on teacher confidence and self-efficacy because many of us need more confidence in our teaching abilities. In my experience, confidence often holds some back from trying something new, like PBL, SEL, and new strategies. This in turn prevents them from growing their teaching practice. Lacking confidence in our teaching can also be emotionally taxing—but it can be overcome with a few simple tweaks to how we plan and deliver our lessons. I also want you and the teachers I coach to get this benefit—which is why we are also focusing on confidence and sound core teaching practice in this chapter.

Lacking confidence as a teacher took a personal toll on me as I struggled immensely to assertively present information during monthly faculty meetings at the schools where I taught, in district meetings as a curriculum specialist, and later in workshops for adult learners. Don't get me wrong, I typically did a good job, but internally I would suffer from anxiety and self-doubt. This was not a good place to be and, in retrospect, wasn't worth the years of hardship. However, by paying close attention to sound core instruction and what I'm experiencing internally (emotionally), I have learned how to make all butterflies fly in the same direction. If I did it, so can you. It just takes practice, a solid foundational framework, and patience with oneself.

To deliver instruction with confidence, it's always important to pay close attention to sound practices for purposefully planning and teaching our lessons. If our core instruction is solid, we'll have a solid foundation for adding to our repertoire—including SEL-infused PBL. This means intentionally leveraging education research and our personal experiences with actionable steps through evidence-based instructional strategies and vetted educational protocols. This is often referred to as our pedagogical strategies (Edsys, 2018) and/or instructional design (Groshell, n.d.) practices for teaching and learning. All teachers should consider these types of items even when designing their PBL lessons, which we will cover in the forthcoming sections.

5 KEY BUILDING BLOCKS OF EFFECTIVE CORE INSTRUCTION

Core or Tier 1 instruction is the critical whole-group lessons teachers produce in primary subject areas that serve as a good backdrop for the differentiation strategies required to support struggling learners and those with diverse needs. Intentional and solid core instruction is critical for PBL, SEL, and other approaches to teaching. For example, a school beginning or enhancing the implementation of tiered instruction as part of a multi-tiered system of supports (MTSS) framework (S. Hurst, 2014) may need guidance in identifying and carrying out the components of Tier 1 instruction (Metcalf, n.d.). Tiers are designed to challenge students at their appropriate ability levels. Similarly, schools looking to use a Response to Intervention (RTI; Shapiro, n.d.) or PBL teaching model may need similar guidance on a good starting point for planning and facilitating lessons in tandem with helping teachers determine their students' learning needs.

But it's not enough for teachers to only have a sound system for planning and facilitating relevant lessons. They also need to monitor student engagement and academic achievement intentionally. This allows for tweaking and refining practice over time from an informed approach. To support the educators I coached, I created a versatile framework to serve as a good starting point for outlining the essential five must-have elements of good core instruction. As we progress through the following chapters and Part 2 of this book, we will consider these following elements as components of our project ideation process. They are therefore featured in our Project and Performance Task Planner (see Appendix A, p. 135).

1. **Relevant evidence-based curriculum.** *Curriculum* refers to an evidence-based (Wing Institute, n.d.), standards, and competency-aligned sequence of planned experiences that help learners capture content concepts and

applied skills that follow local standards, graduate profiles, career skills, SEL, and learners' interests. Teachers designing project unit plans must consider and nail down what kids need to learn and transfer in each project.

Although there's nothing wrong with carrying out core instruction using purchased curriculum and scripted resources, I don't recommend following said resources verbatim. There must be personalization of what you are teaching your unique learners, otherwise we risk losing student engagement (Valenzuela, 2022h) due to lack of relevance. The planner shown in Figure 4.1 allows you to expand project ideas using your curricular resources to design and fine-tune a personalized PBL unit or performance task to fit your class context.

Furthermore, to assist you and your planning teams in designing core instruction in meaningful and compelling ways for kids, try the empathy mapping process (see Chapter 3) in tandem with straightforward backward design planning tools (Valenzuela, 2022b). The former can be powerful for determining relevance for students. The latter is a simple way to map and align learning goals with assessments, lessons, and sound instructional practices. I will model its use later in this chapter.

2. **The promotion of literacy and numeracy skills across subject areas.** Literacy and numeracy skills (Victoria State Government, 2022) are undoubtedly foundational for reading, writing, reasoning, and problem-solving across multiple disciplines. Even if you're not an English language arts or math teacher or utilizing a formal program for tiering and differentiation (e.g., MTSS, RTI, PBL), improving your core instruction should integrate literacy and math in ways that complement your core lessons meaningfully.

For example, science, social science, and elective teachers can highlight the reading and writing skills pertinent to the content they teach. As a science, technology, engineering, and math teacher, I've found that having my students outline the design process steps while paying attention to grammar, sentence structure, and citations significantly improves their literacy skills over time. In PBL, having kids create and rehearse using presentation scripts is also a powerful literacy builder that reinforces their speaking and listening skills (Valenzuela, 2019b).

Non-math teachers can help learners improve their basic knowledge of numbers by embedding numeracy skills into daily lessons in their PBL units. Skills may include building understanding in the following areas:

- Budgeting (Study.com, n.d.)
- Calculations (Cuemath, n.d.)
- Representing and interpreting data (Dacey & Eston, 2003)
- Measurement and data analysis (Tickled Pink in Primary, n.d.)
- Relationships between numbers (Peanut Butter Fish Lessons, n.d.)

3. **High-yielding strategies to facilitate lessons.** When used appropriately, high-yielding strategies (Learning Focused, n.d.) have been shown to produce

positive results in students' academic achievement. Having a set of go-to strategies for boosting critical thinking (Valenzuela, 2022g), cooperative learning (Merrill, 2019), and providing feedback (Valenzuela, 2022c) (among other items) can strengthen core instruction and Tier 2 and 3 interventions. To remove your guesswork, in this book I have purposefully selected and uplifted strategies for implementing SEL and PBL that can produce high-yielding results.

Additionally, researcher Robert Marzano's work simplifies strategy selection because he outlines nine strategies (Technology & Learning, n.d.) to improve student achievement in any grade level or content area. Visible Learning research (Corwin, n.d.-b.) by John Hattie is also a good source for helping educators understand and adapt research to strategy selection in their particular context.

Try various strategies to gain insight into how they help learners succeed. Learn the appropriate times to use them because every strategy shouldn't be used daily or in every lesson and project.

4. **Student engagement and academic achievement monitoring.** Academic research supports (Dyer, 2015) a strong correlation between student engagement and student achievement, which teachers implementing PBL across grade levels and disciplines need to consider as a part of their core and daily instruction. In *Visible Learning*, John Hattie (2009, p. 32) writes, "No manner of school reform will be successful until we first face and resolve the engagement problem." Hattie's advice is essential not just for teachers but also for administrators and district supervisors to consider when implementing new instructional initiatives.

Monitoring student engagement is not difficult, but it must be intentional. Poll Everywhere (n.d.) recommends doing so in the following ways:

- Asking questions and leading discussions
- Observing participation in collaborative work by seeing how students respond in smaller settings
- Polling students using engagement surveys

Here are some good questions inspired by SurveyMonkey (n.d.) for you to consider when anonymously polling your students following PBL experiences:

- Rank this year's lessons and PBL units from easiest to hardest.
- Which activities did you learn from the most in our project?
- What are three things that can improve our next project?
- What is one thing you'd change about our project if you could?
- What advice would you give your teacher as I plan our next class project?
- What are you proud of accomplishing in our last class project?
- What do you want to learn in our next PBL experience?

Academic achievement should be monitored daily using informal and ungraded formative assessments (Edutopia, 2015) throughout projects.

Good assessment tools for strengthening core instruction may include thumbs-up responses (Edutopia, 2019a) and exit tickets. Quizzes, biweekly, end-of-unit, and benchmark assessments are metrics your district may have in place for you to use.

5. **An understanding of your own impact.** Hattie explains the importance of listening to our students to inform us of our impact on their engagement and learning (Professional Learning Supports, 2014); we can also seek feedback from trusted colleagues (Valenzuela, 2022d). When teachers consider themselves learners, it is easier to have conversations with students and colleagues about the areas of our core instruction within PBL units that we can improve.

Excellent practice requires vulnerability and focuses on what's not working with our core teaching and particular students. Seeking the right strategies for improving our impact becomes intentional (see #4) instead of jumping on the latest teaching trend(s) (see #3).

Surveying, polling, and student conferences can help improve teaching impact. You might ask questions such as the following (QuestionPro, n.d.):

- Which classroom activities help you learn most?

- What changes do you recommend I make to help you learn better?

- What motivates you to learn most?

- What can I do better?

- What aspects of projects do you enjoy?

- What would make project work more meaningful to you?

FIGURE 4.1 PROJECT AND PERFORMANCE TASK PLANNER TEMPLATE PREVIEW

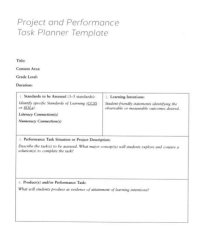

SOURCE: Inspired by GRASP Model by Jay McTighe. By Lifelong Learning Defined, Inc. The full template is available in Appendix A (page 135).

THE PROJECT AND PERFORMANCE TASK PLANNER

The Project and Performance Task Planner is inspired by the GRASP (Goal, Role, Audience, Situation, Products) performance task model by Jay McTighe (Defined Learning, n.d.) and the coaching work I do to support schools. A performance task is a learning activity or assessment that asks students to transfer learning via the performance of either a tangible product or a task that's the follow-through of their knowledge and understanding (Defined Learning, 2015). The Project and Performance Task Planner is also helpful for capturing critical instructional considerations teachers should consider for effective PBL (SEL, authentic audiences, student roles, etc.). In Appendix A, the full Project and Performance Task Planner is available for you to access.

Both projects and performance tasks are excellent for having kids learn complex concepts by exploring and putting their new knowledge to use authentically. Typically, in a full PBL unit, students create two or more products. In a performance task, students generally only create one real-world product, but they can still present it as a public product. Performance tasks typically take less time to complete and allow teachers to develop their skills for PBL while still providing their learners with a deeper learning experience. Educators have the option of both student learning experiences to choose from. To model effective use of the Project and Performance Task Planner, Part 2 of this book features three adaptable SEL-infused projects you may reference as you design your own unique project relevant to your learners.

KEY FEATURES OF THE PLANNER

I've been helping teachers design curricula (lessons and projects) for over a decade. Some enjoy the process while others prefer their time in the classroom instead of planning for it. All in all, most are not fans of prolonged planning. However, teachers need to know what they're teaching from start to finish. This planner highlights what's truly important and removes the fluff and redundancy that planning sometimes entails. To maximize efficiency and brain trust, teachers can opt to design their PBL lessons either individually or with their colleagues—preferably in their grade-level planning teams. In tandem with helping teachers capture the abovementioned essentials of good core instruction and some PBL must-haves, the planner features the following easy-to-complete eight sections related to project/performance task overview and instruction, which we will review together in the text that follows. Sections 9–11 of the planner will be explained in subsequent chapters.

1. **Standards to Be Assessed:** These should include learning derived from local standards, graduate profiles, career skills, SEL, and learners' interests. Non-ELA and math teachers should also make literacy and numeracy connections whenever applicable. To make this simpler to carry out teachers can focus on no more than five standards/competencies per unit plan. To see an example of this section completed, please see Part 2 of this book, on page 69.

2. **Learning Intentions:** The rewriting of the *standards to be addressed* into student-friendly statements identifying the observable or measurable outcomes desired. For example:

- I can explain how human activity affects the health of bodies of water and the ecosystems they support.

- I can collect and analyze data to inform my decisions and design better solutions to real-world problems.

- I can present my conclusions to an audience using multimedia tools that more effectively convey my message.

3. **Performance Task Situation or Project Description:** Describe the task(s) to be assessed and provide details about the major concept(s) students will explore and conjure a solution(s) to complete the task. Situation relates to a performance task and a project description captures what students will do and create during a PBL unit plan. Here are two straightforward examples for you to consider as you develop your own plan:

Performance Task Situation Example

- For this performance task, students will apply computational thinking (*decomposition, abstraction, pattern recognition, and algorithm design*) to create an original program using core coding concepts (*outputs, inputs, loops, functions, variables, and logic*). To complete the task, students will learn from computer science experts, work in teams, and assume the roles of software engineers, software developers, or programmers. Their application will be evaluated for functionality, errors, and gaps and whether the program's outcome matches desired expectations.

Project Description Example

- In this project, students will learn to apply computational thinking (*decomposition, abstraction, pattern recognition, and algorithm design*) to solve computational problems. They will design an original program using core coding concepts (*outputs, inputs, loops, functions, variables, and logic*). Students will also prepare a presentation, either in video or in person, to teach coding skills to an authentic audience comprising of experts and community members. Throughout the project, they will interact with computer science experts, work in teams, and assume the roles of either software engineers, software developers, or programmers.

4. **Product(s) and/or Performance Task(s):** State the product(s) or performance task(s) students will produce as evidence of attainment of the learning intentions. As a reminder, the products students create can also be assessed as a performance task if you opt not to implement an entire project. A performance task is a learning activity or assessment that students perform to transfer their knowledge, understanding, and skillsets. In performance tasks, students produce a tangible product or performance that's evidence of the follow-through of the learning intentions. Please refer to Table 1.1 on page 18 for examples of five different types of products and performance tasks for you to choose from.

5. **Authentic Audience:** The audience is the people to whom students will present their work in the public product. Those viewing student work should be individuals interested in the findings and products that students create. Community members, industry experts, local politicians, parents, and school and district administrators are all examples of authentic audience members. There may be a call to action made by the student

presenter(s) for the audience to assist with the project or help in a cause. I will expand on how students can create good calls to action in Chapter 8 on page 97.

6. **Student Role(s):** A role provides students the opportunity to assume the career or job role associated with accomplishing the goal(s) of the project or performance task. For example, a student working independently to complete a product or performance task may assume the role of a doctor, attorney, intern, computer programmer, and so on. Students working in teams should take roles specific to the context of the products they are developing. For example, a medical team prescribing treatment to sick patients may comprise the head doctor, medical intern, and nurses. A software development team may include a project manager, software developers, and programmers. The goal here is for students to assume a real-world professional role.

7. **Driving Question (DQ):** A DQ is the project's central question used to guide students throughout the learning process and should be introduced on the very first day of the project. Moreover, the DQ also reminds students about what they're aiming to achieve as they work through the project. Good DQs are compelling and articulate the purpose of the project. I recommend developing them in the following four simple steps:

   - Framing words such as *how can*, *should*, *could*, and *what*
   - Identifying the role students assume, such as *engineer*, *lawyer*, *environmental scientist*, and *economist*
   - Articulating action verbs such as *design*, *create*, *develop*, and *showcase*
   - Identifying the intended audience, such as those viewing the public product

   Here are some examples of driving questions designed using the above mentioned four steps:

   - How can we, as software developers, design an app to inform the public about restoration projects in our local area?
   - How can we, as historians, create a virtual historical tour for people new to our region or state?
   - How can we, as environmental scientists, create an infographic to inform members of our community about relevant local ecological concerns?

8. **Instructional Alignment Tool for Student Task Instructions and Teaching:** This tool is inspired by backward design methodology by Jay McTighe and Grant Wiggins but does not replace McTighe's Understanding by Design resources through ASCD (n.d.). Instead, it is a simple table with four columns, quickly allowing educators to map their instruction in alignment with products/performance tasks (also described as summative assessment) and daily learning intentions. It also allows teachers to pace instruction (Valenzuela, 2022b). Here's how to align your instruction in four steps using the planner (see Table 4.1).

TABLE 4.1 INSTRUCTIONAL ALIGNMENT TOOL COMPLETED EXAMPLE

PRODUCT(S) AND TASKS	LEARNING INTENTIONS AND PACING	FORMAL AND INFORMAL FORMATIVE ASSESSMENTS	MINI-LESSONS, HIGH-YIELDING STRATEGIES, AND SCAFFOLDS
Monday–Tuesday: *Sphero Bolt program*	*I can develop a flowchart using step-by-step algorithms of pseudocode for my Sphero Bolt program.*	*Flowchart summary of algorithm logic for program* *Flowchart rubric* *Reflection in design journal* *Exit ticket following daily lesson* *Emotions check-in*	*Computer science guest speaker* *Gliffy article on flowchart universal symbols and Connect, Extend, Challenge* *SEL strategies*
Wednesday– Thursday: *Sphero Bolt program*	*I can define and apply loops in my Sphero Bolt program.*	*Loops quiz* *Loops rubric* *Exit ticket following daily lesson* *Emotions check-in*	*CT elements graphic organizer* *Station rotations using "Workshop Model" structure* *Coding with teacher* *Coding with a peer (pair programming)* *Individual coding* *Sphero programming video* *SEL strategies*
Friday: *Sphero Bolt program*	*I can define and apply conditional logic in my Sphero Bolt program.*	*Program rubric* *Reflection and celebration following presentation* *Emotions check-in*	*Presentation rehearsal* *Program presentation* *SEL strategies*

1. **Column one: Determine product(s) and task(s).** Well-designed summative assessments drive instruction when they align to a standard(s) or a benchmark. The tool should be used to align instruction for summative assessments in the form of products, demonstration of a performance task(s), or literary composition.

   For example, a particular unit or project plan can call students to create written, technology-based, or constructed products (reports, PSAs, model prototypes, etc.). Once you determine what you want your students to do and produce by the end of a specified time, that information goes into column one.

2. **Column two: Compose learning intentions and determine pacing.**
Developing learning intentions for projects is a critical practice that is often
neglected in professional development and, therefore, is often excluded or
not well thought out in curriculum design. Derived from academic
standards and learning frameworks, learning intentions are vital to
teaching and observing learning and are the backbone of lessons.

Good learning intentions drive what students will understand and what
they will be able to accomplish following a lesson or project. They need to
go beyond objectives on our whiteboard or lesson plan and should be
unpacked during mini-lessons as the focal point of the academic
conversation between teachers and students.

I use learning intentions to capture learning goals as statements about what
students can do regarding completing the product or task in column one of
the planning tool. You should also pace how long it will take your learners
to master each of the learning intentions. To update the tool, simply restate
what you've already written in number two of the project planner.
Furthermore, Corwin has powerful resources on how to develop and use
learning intentions across grade levels (Corwin, n.d.-a).

3. **Column three: Develop formative assessments.** Each learning goal in
column two will need formative assessment to check students'
understanding. Teachers can decide on both informal and formal formative
assessments (Formplus, n.d.). I find conducting two formal checks (quizzes,
essays, etc.) for each summative assessment good practice for determining
where students need help, remediation, and challenge.

Informal checks can be used daily between our interactions with students
to determine their instructional needs. Here are two common informal
quick checks we can use daily to determine students' understanding.

- **Hand Signals:** Students giving a thumbs-up indicates they understand the
content enough to continue working, and a thumbs-downs shows they
need more time or further assistance capturing the material. Students
wanting privacy can hold their hand only in plain sight to their teacher
(e.g., close to their chest).

- **Entry and Exit Slips:** Check-ins at the start and end of class can provide
a great opportunity to discover what learners recall and where they may
still be stuck. Entry slips can be a question about the previous day of
learning. Exit slips are provided at the end of class to inform teachers
about student progress and where upcoming lessons need to focus. Here
are some adaptable prompts you can use for slips.

  ○ What two things have you learned well, and what are you still
  struggling to understand?

  ○ What interests you most about the work we are doing?

  ○ Right now, I'm feeling . . .

  ○ Today's lesson was difficult because . . .

  ○ I'm feeling most inspired about . . .

4. **Column four: Lessons, high-yielding strategies, and scaffolds.** High-yielding
strategies and scaffolds are what we reach for to teach a particular lesson—
or, in this case, the learning intention(s) in column two. Learning intentions

require us to explain, clarify, and model. Students will need time to practice—moving from guided (teacher-led) to independent. Use the information in #3 of the previous section to determine what makes a strategy high-yielding and select appropriate ones to teach your PBL lessons for each learning intention.

Gleaning insights from formative assessment (column two) helps us put the appropriate scaffolds and interventions in place by updating column four. For example, to help students with their coding skills, I like structuring their learning using station rotations, allowing them to move between working independently and with the teacher or their peers. Teachers can also use a similar process for differentiating and choosing scaffolds that work best for their students. Common scaffolds in PBL may include but are not limited to the following (Houser, n.d.):

- **Teacher modeling:** Through demonstrations, teachers show students how to complete a task or activity and provide insights into the thought processes of its completion.

- **Sentence stems:** These are great scaffolds for helping learners explain their thoughts and ideas. Sentence stems can be excellent support for English language learners (ELLs). Here are some that I like to use in my classroom:

  - The paragraph states that . . .

  - Overall, what the author is trying to say is . . .

  - I disagree with his/her position because . . .

  - I do not understand what the author wrote in the second paragraph. . . . Can you please help clarify?

- **Graphic organizers:** This visual and graphic display tool created by students depicts the relationships between facts, terms, and ideas within learning a major concept(s). Graphic organizers come in many different forms (hierarchical sets, descriptive or thematic maps, flow charts, etc.).

- **Connect to previous knowledge:** When planning the entry event for a project, consider what background knowledge students might have about a concept they can connect to. For example, you can show them a picture or text related to their new learning and ask them if they have any prior experience with the topic.

- **Use of first language:** If your ELLs' first language can improve learning the content you teach, use it as a scaffold. Only translate parts of lessons such as essential vocabulary words, connections between concepts, and step-by-step task instructions.

The knowledge in this chapter will give teachers a lot to consider about their project and lesson planning and overall instructional design practices for teaching and learning. A lot goes into becoming a skilled curriculum developer and facilitator of knowledge—it doesn't happen overnight. When I first began developing my pedagogical strategies for planning and facilitating, I found the systematic approach of using tools and frameworks empowering because of the repetitiveness of it all.

I eventually became more confident because I saw evidence of students grasping concepts and transferring them verbally and physically into practice and expertise.

SUMMARY

· ·

This is a powerful chapter for putting the science of teaching and learning into practical steps educators can take to plan and deliver relevant curricula for their unique students. Using the components of good core instruction and the Project and Performance Task Planner found in this chapter will improve your PBL teaching and understanding of sound teaching and learning. It is my hope that you refer to it as often as you need to continue the learning. Remember, a relevant curriculum entails more than just designing the best project articulating content standards and learning intentions. We must also figure out how to frame what we teach to match the context of the students we teach and then use the teaching strategies that will engage and help them achieve academically. Now that we have a way to organize our SEL-infused projects, the next chapter will complete our learning of the PBL+ Framework by using frequent feedback cycles to guide student work and assessment in PBL.

CHAPTER 5

ELEMENT 5: USE FREQUENT FEEDBACK CYCLES TO GUIDE STUDENT WORK

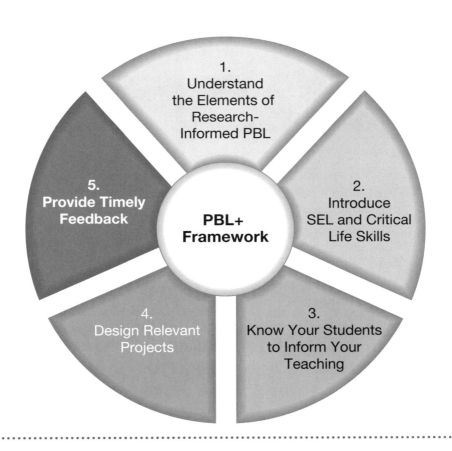

To solidify the PBL+ Framework and support the elements in the previous chapters, we will now structure student work time using frequent feedback cycles. Feedback cycles are used in project-based learning (PBL) to ensure learners are on track with the intended knowledge and skills articulated in the learning intentions. Feedback cycles are powerful because feedback doesn't only have to come from teachers—in PBL, students also learn to provide one another feedback. Remember, the PBL+ Framework is designed to help you implement academic, social, and emotional learning. Therefore, feedback cycles are an integral assessment component PBL teachers can use to provide students with clear guidelines for refining their work throughout the project process.

To bring this to fruition seamlessly, we will learn the power of having students complete their work in drafts, followed by a feedback protocol utilized as a formative assessment checkpoint. Ideally, each project or performance task you facilitate should have three to four feedback cycles to support academics and social and emotional learning (SEL). Keeping in mind that feedback cycles are a form of formative assessment, this chapter will also cover assessment in PBL in the forthcoming pages. The previous chapter taught us that effective PBL requires attention to pedagogical skills and careful planning. To ensure teaching with PBL is implemented with fidelity, readers will learn how to assess PBL using a classroom-tested framework and process.

LEARNING INTENTIONS

▶ Readers will be able to

- consider the importance of feedback to student learning and how to implement frequent feedback cycles into projects and performance tasks,
- use a single-point rubric for improving student work,
- implement a feedback protocol for providing timely feedback, and
- understand the various forms of assessment and how it works in PBL.

FEEDBACK CAN BOOST CONFIDENCE FOR BOTH TEACHERS AND STUDENTS

When I began teaching, I didn't have the confidence I have today. Wanting to do a good job teaching, I was always eager to receive feedback and sought it from my supervisors and colleagues I worked closely with. Unfortunately, some of the feedback I received then either didn't come at all—other than my annual evaluation—or didn't come from a good place. Feedback was often just praise that did little to help me improve my teaching. I needed to understand better what to do with feedback and in structured ways to provide and receive it so it could be actionable. In my coaching work with schools throughout the last 15 years, I am increasingly seeing that this is the reality of many of today's teachers. To build confidence and teaching expertise in their faculty, administrators should invest time in learning to provide their teachers with better feedback (Valenzuela, 2022d). Teachers should also consider how to do the same for their students.

Just as I struggled to receive the feedback I needed as a young and impressionable teacher, I also spent most of my K–12 school experience not receiving the feedback I truly needed. Unfortunately, not receiving feedback in my youth negatively impacted my confidence, self-esteem, and overall quality of my schoolwork. As the years and my insight have progressed, I've realized that my students also struggled to get reliable feedback from me—it's an unfortunate cycle. Many learners need to learn how to request and receive feedback from their teachers and also from peers. If this is the case in your classroom, this chapter will help you develop feedback cycles using practical and evidence-based steps.

FEEDBACK IN PBL

A big part of being a teacher is giving students the right kind of feedback. Although there are many ways of providing students feedback, we must ensure it's kind, targeted, and actionable. I'm a proponent of education researcher John Hattie's view of feedback (Visible Learning, n.d.). He said, "While teachers see feedback as corrections, criticism, comments, and clarifications, for students unless it includes 'where-to-next' information, they tend to not use it." I encourage you to learn more about John Hattie and his Visible Learning work through Corwin.

Learners, therefore, need feedback they understand and can readily act upon along the continuum of the learning process. As the biggest stakeholder, students must be involved and invested in the feedback. Whether facilitating a PBL unit or a performance task, I prefer to hold projects for two to three weeks and for my students to complete their products in three to four drafts using straightforward rubrics and critique protocols. A critique protocol is a structured process that guides students in giving and receiving meaningful feedback for improving their work (Edutopia, 2016). Critique protocols (also known as feedback protocols) are used in PBL in frequent cycles to help guide student work by draft.

To activate frequent feedback cycles (opportunities), I suggest teachers spend less time on lengthy whole-group lessons and instead work with smaller groups to model, remediate gaps in previous learning, and reteach vital concepts as needed. There, you can manage your lessons, tasks, activities, and learning in the following four-step process within a workshop model–inspired structure (Emerich France, 2020):

- Mini-lesson (10–15 minutes)

- Work time and reflection (35 minutes)

- Feedback protocol (10–15 minutes)

- More work time for either revision or continuing to the next draft and reflection (35 minutes).

  These timings are for two class periods at 50 minutes each. Adjust time frames depending on the length of your teaching block.

A workshop structure is not the only way to teach projects, but it's very conducive to group work, remediation for struggling learners, and frequent feedback loops. Visit the Minds in Bloom website to view a visual representation and for tips on how workshops can be set up (Lynette & Noack, n.d.).

On a personal note, implementing workshops was initially clunky in my classroom—it wasn't perfect, nor is it always. Through repetitive practice, it's become a structure I use successfully to keep learning organized and evaluate students' work as they use feedback to revise their drafts. This practice uses scripted educational protocols with influences that positively affect student learning, as ranked and supported by Hattie's Visible Learning research (Corwin, n.d.-b.).

For example, practices affirmed by Hattie's work (Bruyckere, 2019), such as small-group learning, evaluation and reflection (Pivot, n.d.), and strategies emphasizing feedback, are shown to affect students' learning positively and can support them in completing products in drafts. The caveat here is that teachers will need to model the strategies frequently and in ways that help learners accurately understand performance expectations and how to seek assistance when they don't. Over time they can become more independent learners by giving them the right tools to participate in their own rescue. The following sections will provide two tools we can use to give our students better feedback and for improving their products while working on drafts. These two tools can also be used to assess product and performance task quality.

SINGLE-POINT RUBRICS

Be sure to establish the why for feedback with students early on. For the teacher, feedback is vital to ensure that students produce their best work that can be used to assess their learning accurately. For students, feedback allows them to revise and clarify their understanding before summative judgment by their teachers or the authentic audience at the end of the unit. Above all, feedback helps all learners receive support and additional perspectives on improving any work. Articulating the purpose of feedback is an essential first step in promoting buy-in from students who might otherwise not take it seriously. Having a quality tool at their disposal to jumpstart dialogue around requesting and providing feedback can make all the difference in shifting hearts and minds.

Learners requesting and discussing feedback is critical for acting on it. For that, we'll need an easy-to-use tool. Single-point rubrics (SPRs) are great for getting kids to discuss their learning. An SPR displays criteria for a single level of achievement and also includes an open space for feedback, goal setting, or evidence. SPRs can be used for evaluation and reflection during critique protocols. As mentioned earlier in this chapter, critique protocols follow a structured process that guides students in giving and receiving timely feedback for refining their products (Edutopia, 2016). In the following section, I will outline a critique protocol tool I created for my workshops and list a few good ones you can also use for your feedback cycles on page 61.

SPRs are easy to design because they only have the criteria descriptors in the Proficient column completed. Furthermore, the Proficient column articulates the learning intentions for a specific product or task, as doing so creates alignment between lessons and work time for learners. This particular SPR adaptation has four columns with the following headers (see Tables 5.1 and 5.2):

- Emerging
- Proficient
- Highly Proficient
- Score

TABLE 5.1 SINGLE-POINT RUBRIC TEMPLATE

EMERGING	PROFICIENT	HIGHLY PROFICIENT	
1–3	4	5	
Provide feedback for improvement	Grade-level expectations met Provide feedback for improvement	Provide feedback for improvement	SCORE
	I can . . . (content standard)		/5
	I can . . . (content standard)		/5
	I can . . . (content standard)		/5
	I can . . . (content standard)		/5
Total			/20
Student Reflection: *Following implementation, describe how the performance task can be improved.*			

TABLE 5.2   SINGLE-POINT RUBRIC TEMPLATE COMPLETED EXAMPLE

EMERGING	PROFICIENT	HIGHLY PROFICIENT	
1–3	4	5	
Provide feedback for improvement	Grade-level expectations met Provide feedback for improvement	Provide feedback for improvement	SCORE
	I can develop a flowchart using step-by-step algorithms of pseudocode for my computer program. (CS Standard 7.2)		/5
	I can define and apply loops in my computer program. (CS Standard 7.1 a)		/5
	I can define and apply conditional logic in my computer program. (CS Standard 7.1 a)		/5
	I can present my computer program and its functionality to an audience of experts and community members. (CS Standards 7.1 a, b, 7.2)		/5
Total			/20

The Emerging and Highly Proficient columns begin blank, allowing students ample space to audit their own practice and receive more helpful feedback that addresses critical problem areas and notable areas of excellence. Teachers can leverage this as an opportunity to conference with students about their learning and steps they can take to improve. Similarly, the Score column is also blank, and a five-point grading scale can be completed for each learning goal. Remind students that scores are definitive and are only meant to help them improve and attain their personal best work.

Moreover, they don't have to go at it alone. A collaborative classroom environment is a key to effective PBL instruction. One of the ways to embed collaboration into class culture is to have students provide each other with timely and resourceful feedback—a tool like this SPR can be a good starting point and conversation starter. However, grading can be tricky for students or adults who aren't teachers. I recommend teachers initially model grading for kids—with repetition using the tool, they'll improve over time.

STRUCTURED-FEEDBACK PROTOCOL STEPS AND TOOL

Since students in PBL work together, it is essential to ensure they participate in feedback protocols to provide each other feedback—preferably in cycles and by draft, as discussed in this chapter. Asking students to provide each other with feedback without providing them the resources and structures needed to do so sets them up for failure. Critiquing a peer's work can be entirely new and even stressful for many learners. Undoubtedly, teachers attempting this for the first time will have concerns about the quality of feedback their students provide each other as they fear their students either don't know what to say or will use unhelpful statements like "that's good" or "that's bad."

To move them past surface-level commitment takes structure, using sentence stems, time, and practice. Students must learn to become equal partners in assessment facilitated by frequent feedback cycles. To empower them, we can use structured critique protocols for providing and facilitating feedback through a step-by-step, easy-to-use process. By breaking the feedback process down into actionable steps, protocols create invitations for students to provide helpful feedback in a scaffolded and actionable way.

Protocols like TAG Feedback for K–5 (Edutopia, 2019b), Gallery Walk (Teacher Toolkit, n.d.), Critical Friends (National School Reform Faculty [NSRF], n.d.), and Charrette (School Reform Initiative [SRI], 2017) can be adapted as a form of assessment to help students fine-tune their products and performance tasks in drafts. Critique Protocol by EL Education (n.d.-b) is my personal favorite. I used it to inspire the five steps I use to scaffold the process for students taking turns requesting and providing feedback. Similarly, these are the same steps teachers take in my workshops to provide and receive feedback on their PBL units—it's a very versatile assessment tool. Here are the steps:

Step 1: The presenter explains their product draft and requests feedback while their peer(s) listens (2 minutes). Good norms to lift up here are for the presenter to use language from the learning intentions(s) they're addressing and for the peer listening to take notes. Students more experienced with the feedback process can also grade and complete the empty columns in an SPR.

Step 2: The audience asks the presenter clarifying questions for supporting their feedback. The presenter should respond.

Step 3: To begin with glows, the audience shares what they saw and heard that was in alignment with the performance expectations. The presenter listens.

Step 4: The audience shares concerns about the lack of follow-through of performance expectations or needs for further improvement. The presenter listens and can also update the SPR or take notes.

Step 5: Finally, the audience shares ideas and resources for improving the product drafts. The presenter can take notes and respond.

You can access a kid-friendly short version of the feedback protocol for you to use in your classroom (see Figure 5.1).

FIGURE 5.1 FEEDBACK PROTOCOL TOOL

PROCESS	TIME	PERSON(S)
Presentation The presenter presents their product draft and requests feedback; the audience listens and takes notes.	2 Minutes	Presenter
Clarification The audience asks clarifying questions for supporting their feedback; the presenter makes clarifications.	1 Minute	Audience
"I Saw . . . " The audience shares what they saw in alignment with the performance expectations; the presenter listens.	2 Minutes	Audience
"I Wonder . . . " The audience shares concerns (lacks follow-through of the performance expectations or needs further development); the presenter listens.	2 Minutes	Audience
"Consider using . . ." The audience shares ideas and resources for improving the product draft; the presenter listens and may respond.	3 Minutes	Audience
Total	10 Minutes	

online resources 🖑 Available for download at resources.corwin.com/ProjectBasedLearning+

This tool is no different from the other tools provided in this book—expect their use to be challenging initially. Model its use and allow students time to practice. Encourage them to use the sentence stems of "I saw," "I wonder," and "Consider using" to help them begin providing feedback through kind dialogue. You may even see gradual improvements in how they address one another—which isn't bad. Using the protocol does create longer work time on the front end but will allow for deeper learning and discussions as they master the process. Remember, repetition is the mother of skill.

ASSESSMENT IN PBL

When coaching teachers through their project ideation, many ask me about assessment in PBL—is it different from regular everyday teaching? Since PBL isn't considered by some to be a traditional instructional approach, I understand the question. However, let's reflect for a moment on the learning in the previous chapters with the following questions:

1. Is PBL a research-informed instructional approach?

2. Are we actively learning about our students in order to make the absolute best instructional decisions?

3. Are we concerned with our core instruction and general good teaching practice?

These questions can be answered with a simple yes or no—they're not meant to be complex. If you confidently answered yes to these, know that we need to be very intentional about assessment in PBL and performance tasks using a few simple guidelines (see below). Also, remember that the purpose of assessment is to help students improve their work. If how we assess students confuses, frustrates, or doesn't empower them, we will need to refine our approach. First, I'd like to clarify our understanding of assessment and the types of assessment.

1. **Summative Assessment:** Teachers use summative assessments to evaluate student learning, skill acquisition, and academic achievement following a clearly defined block of instruction—such as at the end of a project, unit plan, course, semester, program, or school year (Glossary of Education Reform, 2013). In PBL, the products and performance tasks students create are summative assessments because they are often evaluated for a final grade at the end of the project or task.

2. **Formative Assessment:** Refers to various methods teachers use to actively evaluate student comprehension, learning needs, and academic progress during lessons, projects, or units. Formative assessment data should be used to improve teaching during the learning process (Glossary of Education Reform, 2014). Using formal and informal formative assessments throughout the learning process empowers teachers to identify gaps in student learning, where they are stuck, and essential concepts in the standards that may need reteaching. Understanding formative assessment in tandem with knowing their students enables teachers to adjust lessons, differentiate instruction, and support learners with the just-right supports necessary for academic achievement.

3. **Formal vs. Informal Formative Assessment:** This difference is very simple but can sometimes trip teachers up. Formal formative assessment refers to evaluation to monitor students' knowledge for a grade—for example, quizzes, written assignments, exams, and essays. Informal formative assessment refers to student evaluation without formal grading—meaning nothing goes in your grade book—examples may include hand signals and entry and exit slips (see Chapter 4, page 51 for more details).

GOOD ASSESSMENT PRACTICES IN PBL

Here are some general, but very straightforward, good rules of thumb when planning assessment during projects and performance tasks:

1. The products and tasks students complete are a form of **summative assessment** and will be the final grade you enter in your grade book at the end of the project.

2. For every summative assessment, provide students with at least two **formal formative assessment** opportunities. This will ensure you are better aware of how your learners grasp the intended knowledge and skills outlined in the daily learning intentions.

3. Do not grade students for group work—only individual work. This can be done by assigning them roles and specific tasks to complete—thus allowing them only to be graded for the actual work they complete. This is a critical practice and will be explained in more detail in Chapter 10 on page 119.

4. Commonly, students and outside experts provide students **feedback** as they work on their product drafts. They may even use the grading system in the previously mentioned SPR as part of their feedback (see Table 5.2). Although there's nothing wrong with having multiple eyes on a piece of work during the draft refinement process, only the teacher should assess for grades that end up in the grade book. This means that only teachers should carry out formal formative assessments.

Suppose you have already determined that the various types of assessment are elegantly categorized in the Project and Performance Task Planner for your convenience. In that case, you are already in tune with the power of PBL+. The purpose is to assist you with executing PBL through the lens of research-informed and timeless pedagogy that you may also apply when you're not teaching projects.

SUMMARY

This chapter closes Part 1 of this book. It solidifies the PBL+ Framework by implementing frequent feedback cycles to improve student work and the role of assessment during the project process. This framework is a result of numerous workshop surveys over a decade by teachers like you who informed me what they need to be more confident about teaching PBL and SEL using sound pedagogical strategies. Now that we have solid knowledge about PBL, SEL, and how we want to implement projects and performance tasks, we will move into Part 2 of this book to explore adaptable SEL-themed projects.

PART 2

. . . .

SEL-INFUSED PROJECTS

Part 2 provides three adaptable social and emotional learning (SEL)-infused projects that exemplify the power of the PBL+ student-centered approach to teaching—all of which can be customized for the students in any class. This section also provides examples of aligning SEL competencies with career learning and content standards to ensure students' learning is relevant and rigorous. Additionally, the exemplar projects in this section provide examples of how you can scaffold your approach to PBL+ to provide your learners with the necessary tools and strategies to improve their SEL skills at their own pace. When applied correctly, this gradual approach helps ensure that no matter what PBL+ looks like in your classroom, you'll set yourself and your students up for improvements every time.

CHAPTER 6

....

UNDERSTANDING SELF-AWARENESS FOR CONNECTING PASSION AND PURPOSE

Self-awareness is an essential social and emotional learning (SEL) skill youth can use to continuously improve in their own personal growth. Self-awareness provides learners with deeper insight into themselves—this is called knowledge of self. Think of knowledge of self as who we are and self-awareness as what we do (Waters, 2022). Moreover, self-awareness can be leveraged for living a more authentic life to one's true nature because we energetically pursue topics that interest us and compel us to become actively engaged. Not only can having more self-awareness boost students' creativity and confidence (Waters, 2022), but it can also improve their future career choices, such as job-related well-being (Sutton et al., 2015) and job satisfaction (Wexley et al., 1980). A project that harnesses their self-awareness for connecting passion to purpose can jumpstart kids to a fulfilled future.

WHY STUDENTS NEED TO IMPROVE SELF-AWARENESS

Chapter 2 explored the CASEL 5 competencies for SEL as the central focus of our PBL+ teaching. We also discussed the urgent need for SEL to emotionally support today's students due to the catastrophic effects of COVID-19 and the challenges many are experiencing at home (Centers for Disease Control and Prevention, 2021). Additionally, many of them express being dissatisfied with school (Harvard Business Publishing, 2022). Current conditions burden educators, with many needing assistance with practical ways of helping students requiring emotional and academic support. Using PBL+ projects emphasizing social and emotional health and academic learning is one research-backed method we can use. According to Fuligni and Galván (2022), co-directors at the UCLA Center for the Developing Adolescent, it's imperative for young people to participate in experiences that can boost their mental health.

Fuligni and Galván (2022) point to three decades of research, primarily in neuroscience and developmental psychology, suggesting that exposing youth experiencing mental health issues to conditions and experiences that have proven to help youngsters thrive and do well emotionally, socially, and academically can be beneficial. Specifically, they recommend having youth engage in activities schools can support to promote the following:

- Trying new things in an environment conducive to learning and exploration
- Improving the lives of others
- Healthy relationships with adults—including family and in the community

Bearing these items in mind, this chapter is about taking what we know works and empowering teachers to help learners use their self-awareness skills and a detailed research-informed process to make themselves happier and more fulfilled at school by exploring, discovering, and excelling at their passions and interests. This level of self-awareness can also help connect them to a larger sense of purpose, as having passion and interest in topics they find compelling and having a meaningful purpose can be strong indicators of lasting fulfillment and positive mindsets (Valenzuela, 2023). Furthermore, the adaptable exemplar project in this chapter aims to help you provide your students with the self-awareness skills needed to learn ways to support and self-manage themselves.

THE SELF-AWARENESS PROJECT: CONNECTING PASSION TO PURPOSE
Project Description

Young people can live fulfilled lives if they discover what makes them happy and compels them to become the best possible version of themselves. This project allows youth to develop greater self-awareness skills by exploring and connecting their passions and interests to the purpose of making a difference in their communities by helping others. Students begin by brainstorming what makes them happy and compels them to learn and act. They will also identify their passions and interest and steps they can take to build expertise in a chosen topic. Mapping their own journey, they will then use what they learn to design a solution for someone or an entity in their community that needs their expertise. To execute their self-awareness project plans, students will identify problems of practice and develop a framework of change along with how-to steps that will be taught to their intended audience for its implementation.

> Important Note for Teachers: It's common knowledge that typically, in project-based learning (PBL), learners collaborate with their peers in teams. Given this project's focus on self-awareness to connect passion with purpose, some students will want to work alone. There is no rule that all students must work together. Allow them to cultivate their passion or interest individually if they'd like to.

Project Duration and Grade Levels

- Approximately 3 weeks
- Grade Level: Middle to high school (6–12)

Driving Question (DQ)

- Because students will be exploring their own interests and passions, they will develop their unique DQ. They may work individually or with a peer(s). Here are some DQ sentence starters for them to consider:

  1. *How do I, as an _____, create _____ about _____?* (e.g., "How do I, as an artificial intelligence specialist, develop an AI-powered solution addressing the unique needs of a client?")

  2. *How do we, as _____, create _____ about _____?* (e.g., "How do we, as artificial intelligence specialists, develop an AI-powered solution addressing the unique needs of a client?")

  3. *How can I use _____ to demonstrate _____?* (e.g., "How can I use multimedia effectively to demonstrate the role of photosynthesis in plant health?")

  4. *How can we use _____ to demonstrate _____?* (e.g., "How can we use multimedia effectively to demonstrate the role of photosynthesis in plant health?")

Content Standards and SEL Connections

- **CCSS.ELA-Literacy.SL.9-10.4:** Present information, findings, and supporting evidence clearly, concisely, and logically such that listeners can follow the line of reasoning and the organization, development, substance, and style are appropriate to purpose, audience, and task.

- **CCSS.ELA-Literacy.W.11-12.2:** Write informative/explanatory texts to examine and convey complex ideas, concepts, and information clearly and accurately through the effective selection, organization, and analysis of content.

- **CCSS.Math.Content.HSN-Q.A.1:** Use units as a way to understand problems and to guide the solution of multistep problems; choose and interpret units consistently in formulas; choose and interpret the scale and the origin in graphs and data displays.

- **CCSS.Math.Content.HSN-Q.A.2:** Define appropriate quantities for the purpose of descriptive modeling.

- **SEL Connection(s):** Self-awareness includes a growth mindset, understanding blind spots, asking appropriate questions, seeking assistance, listening to feedback, being open to change, and seeking to help others.

- **Literacy Connection(s):** Reading and writing, analyzing and evaluating text, summarizing and synthesizing information. Writing clear and coherent sentences, using appropriate grammar, spelling, and punctuation. Developing ideas and supporting them with evidence. Organizing and presenting writing logically and effectively. Speaking and listening, articulating thoughts and ideas clearly and effectively, active listening and comprehension, using gestures, body language, and tone to enhance communication. Asking questions to clarify and seek information. Participating in presentations. Giving and receiving feedback. Understanding and using nonverbal cues. Using Standard English and appropriate language for the audience. Adapting speech for different audiences.

- **Numeracy Connection(s):** Making sense of problems and persevering in solving them, modeling with mathematics, attending to precision, looking for and making use of structure.

Learning Intentions

1. I can examine and identify my passions and interests following the directions in my 5-step organizer.

2. I can organize my findings and evidence in my 5-step organizer to support my passion and interests.

3. I can organize my content in my 5-step organizer effectively to ensure clarity and accuracy about solving a problem(s) of practice for a specific person or entity.

4. I can identify an expert(s) who can mentor and coach me as I build expertise to solve a problem of practice.

5. I can communicate what self-awareness means and how it pertains to making myself happy and fulfilled.

6. I can build expertise in my passion or interest to solve a problem of practice and develop a model-of-change framework for others to use to achieve similar success.

7. I can write informative/explanatory texts and include mathematical modeling to examine and convey the steps in my framework or model of change.

8. I can select appropriate audience members who will benefit most from my presentation information.

9. I can develop my presentation to be appropriate for my audience and explain my framework or model of change.

10. I can present information clearly and concisely to ensure listeners understand the reasoning behind my findings in my framework or model of change.

11. I can use appropriate language and tone in my presentation to engage my audience.

Final Products With Details

1. **Passion to Purpose 5-Step Organizer:** The teacher guides students through discovering their passion (or an interest) and turning it into purpose through various activities. The steps involve:

   - Identifying a passion or topic of interest.

   - Finding a problem of practice related to your passion or interest.

   - Setting a goal to solve the problem of practice and working with experts to develop a solution.

   - Creating a framework or model of change to assist others in solving a similar problem of practice in their community.

2. **Framework or Model of Change:** Students will design an original framework or model of change to organize problem-solving approaches based on their goal(s) and knowledge. The student-developed framework or model must present a visual representation of the theory of the problem, theory of action, and logic model that can guide others with similar pursuits. Additionally, students will map backward from the intended outcomes to highlight necessary elements and details others must know to achieve similar success.

3. **Public Presentation:** Students will, independently or with peers, conduct a public presentation of their framework or model of change. They will:

   - Prepare a clear and concise explanation of the problem of practice and the need for a framework or model of change.

   - Use visual aids to help represent and illustrate essential elements and components in their framework.

   - Present the framework and related steps in a logical and organized manner.

   - Demonstrate how the framework can be adapted to help others with similar goals and pursuits achieve success.

   - Engage the audience through modeling, explanation, and questions and answers.

Phase 1: Compelling Hook and Initial Teacher Lessons

The compelling hook launches the project to engage learners. Learn more about the significance of the compelling hook in PBL in Chapter 9 on page 107. To help provide a solid foundation for completing the Passion to Purpose 5-Step Organizer, the teacher facilitates a mini-lesson on each step in the document (access the document using the lesson resources on page 73). To apply this knowledge, students engage in prescribed activities to identify a passion or interest they wish to cultivate. Students who are having a difficult time identifying a passion or interest can look for ways to add service to others or an entity in their school or community. Upon settling on their topic, students draft their DQ for the project. The DQ will lead to other questions that eventually translate into the topics they research and design their projects around.

Phase 1: Instructional Alignment Tool

PRODUCT(S) AND TASKS	LEARNING INTENTIONS AND PACING	FORMAL AND INFORMAL FORMATIVE ASSESSMENTS	MINI-LESSONS, HIGH-YIELDING STRATEGIES, AND SCAFFOLDS
Passion to Purpose 5-Step Organizer **(3–4 class periods)**	I can examine and identify my passions and interests following the directions in my 5-step organizer (1–2 class periods)	• Written reflection on 5-step organizer • Responses during classroom discussions • Exit ticket	• Teacher-led mini-lesson explaining major concepts • Videos explaining passion and providing service to others • Introduction to *Passion to Purpose 5-Step Organizer* • All-class discussion and debrief
	I can organize my findings and evidence in my 5-step organizer to support my passion and interests (2 class periods)	• Written reflection on 5-step organizer • Feedback protocol using rubric • Checklist • Exit ticket	• Teacher directions and guiding questions • *Passion to Purpose 5-Step Organizer* • Teacher/student feedback
	I can organize my content in my 5-step organizer effectively to ensure clarity and accuracy about solving a problem(s) of practice for a specific person or entity (1 class period)	• Teacher-led discussion • Written explanation • Feedback protocol using rubric • Checklist • Exit ticket	• Teacher directions and guiding questions • Additional resources pertaining to specific problem(s) • *Passion to Purpose 5-Step Organizer* • Teacher/student feedback
	I can identify an expert(s) who can mentor and coach me as I build expertise to solve a problem of practice (1 class period)	• Written reflection on 5-step organizer • Discussion with teacher • Exit ticket	• Individual and small-group teaching • Additional resources pertaining to specific expert(s) • Teacher/student feedback • *Passion to Purpose 5-Step Organizer*

PRODUCT(S) AND TASKS	LEARNING INTENTIONS AND PACING	FORMAL AND INFORMAL FORMATIVE ASSESSMENTS	MINI-LESSONS, HIGH-YIELDING STRATEGIES, AND SCAFFOLDS
	I can communicate what self-awareness means and how it pertains to making myself happy and fulfilled (1 class period)	• Teacher-led discussion • Written and oral explanation • Poster presentation	• Working in pairs • Poster template • Teacher/student feedback • *Passion to Purpose 5-Step Organizer*

Important Note: Teachers can develop their *passion to purpose* mini-lesson using the following two resources.

LESSON RESOURCES

USING SEL TO GUIDE STUDENTS FROM PASSION TO PURPOSE ARTICLE

https://edut.to/3jutQzy

PBL+ PASSION TO PURPOSE 5-STEP ORGANIZER

https://bit.ly/3l5xlNo

To read a QR code, you must have a smartphone or tablet with a camera. We recommend that you download a QR code reader app that is made specifically for your phone or tablet brand.

Phase 2: Building Expertise and Developing the Framework or Model of Change

With their topic, background knowledge, and goal in place, students can either work individually or join a team with peers interested in the same passion or interest topic. They will meet with an expert (virtually or in person) their teacher vets to begin researching the problem of practice and start conjuring up solutions. Once a viable solution is identified and tested, the students will design a framework or model of change to highlight necessary elements and details others with similar pursuits can implement to achieve similar results. The framework or model must present a visual representation of the problem, a theory of action, and a logic model that can guide others. A group poster that can be created using edtech tools is shared during a feedback protocol to display their framework or model (Adobe Express and Google Draw are possible tools). This feedback informs how to improve their work in preparation for the final product (public presentation). Teachers will need to facilitate two mini-lessons to teach learners the major components of a framework or model of change and mathematical modeling.

Phase 2: Instructional Alignment Tool

PRODUCT(S) AND TASKS	LEARNING INTENTIONS AND PACING	FORMAL AND INFORMAL FORMATIVE ASSESSMENTS	MINI-LESSONS, HIGH-YIELDING STRATEGIES, AND SCAFFOLDS
Framework or Model of Change (5–7 class periods)	I can build expertise in my passion or interest to solve a problem of practice and develop a framework or model of change for others to use to achieve similar success (3 class periods)	• Written reflection • *Framework or Model of Change* template • Feedback protocol using rubric • Exit ticket	• Teacher-led mini-lesson explaining major concepts • Videos and articles explaining the essential features of a framework or model of change • Introduction to the *Framework or Model of Change* template • Teacher/student feedback
	I can write informative/explanatory texts and include mathematical modeling to examine and convey the steps in my framework or model of change (2–3 class periods)	• Descriptive text in the *Framework or Model of Change* template • Feedback protocol using rubric • Checklist • Exit ticket	• Teacher-led mini-lesson explaining mathematical modeling • Resources on mathematical modeling • *Framework or Model of Change* template • Teacher/student feedback

Important Note: Teachers can develop their *framework or model of change* and mathematical modeling mini-lessons using the following resources.

DEVELOPING A
FRAMEWORK OR
MODEL OF CHANGE
CHECKLIST

https://bit.ly/3Y1TqLg

MATHEMATICAL
MODELING LESSON
PLANS

https://bit.ly/3Xa9MQU

ADOBE EXPRESS

https://adobe.ly/3YkwvKL

Phase 3: Preparing Students for the Public Presentation

Before the public presentation event, students should rehearse their speaking points and how they plan to showcase their information at least three times in class. Teachers should encourage them to practice at home as it will allow them to deliver their speaking points more confidently on presentation day. Getting rubric-based feedback is essential to the PBL+ process and helps them execute their possible work. Before presenting, the students will identify and select audience members they feel will benefit most from the information they put forward and invite them to attend the public presentation. Teachers will need to go through the appropriate protocols in their school building to coordinate the event. During the session, students will engage with the public and guide them through the concepts and content of their framework or model of change while answering questions that elucidate their ideas. After they present, students should reflect with their teacher to discuss their growth and challenges and set goals for future projects.

Phase 3: Instructional Alignment Tool

PRODUCT(S) AND TASKS	LEARNING INTENTIONS AND PACING	FORMAL AND INFORMAL FORMATIVE ASSESSMENTS	MINI-LESSONS, HIGH-YIELDING STRATEGIES, AND SCAFFOLDS
Public Presentation **(3–4 class periods)**	I can select appropriate audience members who will benefit most from my presentation information (1 class period)	• Written notes and reflection • Responses during classroom discussions • Exit ticket	• Teacher-led mini-lesson explaining major concepts • Videos showcasing presentations • All-class discussion and debrief

(Continued)

(Continued)

PRODUCT(S) AND TASKS	LEARNING INTENTIONS AND PACING	FORMAL AND INFORMAL FORMATIVE ASSESSMENTS	MINI-LESSONS, HIGH-YIELDING STRATEGIES, AND SCAFFOLDS
	I can develop my presentation to be appropriate for my audience and explain my framework or model of change (3 class periods)	• Feedback protocol using rubric • Presentation checklist • Exit ticket	• Teacher directions and guiding questions • Presentation app (e.g., PowerPoint) • Teacher/student feedback
	I can present information clearly and concisely to ensure listeners understand the reasoning behind my findings in my framework or model of change (3 class periods)	• Teacher-led discussion • Feedback protocol using rubric • Checklist • Exit ticket	• Individual and small-group rehearsal • Additional resources pertaining to presentations • Presentation app • Teacher/student feedback
	I can use appropriate language and tone in my presentation to engage my audience (3 class periods)	• Written notes • Discussion with teacher	• Individual and small-group rehearsal • Additional resources pertaining to specific expert(s) • Teacher/student feedback

Important Note: Teachers can develop their facilitation skills and have students use single-point rubrics by accessing the full Passion to Purpose PBL+ Project Template in Appendix A.

CHAPTER 7

....

UNDERSTANDING SOCIAL AWARENESS FOR HAVING SUCCESSFUL RELATIONSHIPS

Theoretical physicist Albert Einstein (2010) once said, "Peace cannot be kept by force; it can only be achieved by understanding" (p. 252). Making an effort to understand others and how they feel is an intricate component of good social awareness for belonging and navigating the social aspects of school and work. According to social psychology, belonging is an intrinsic motivation to join with others and be socially accepted (Kenrick et al., 2010). For human interactions to be successful, social awareness and its wide range of skills such as empathy, communication, and respect (among other skills) are the prerequisite. Furthermore, social-awareness skills are also required for establishing and maintaining successful and synergistic relationships.

STUDENTS CAN IMPROVE SOCIAL-AWARENESS SKILLS IN TANDEM WITH ACADEMIC CONTENT

My personal and professional experiences interacting with others led me to conclude that relationships are among life's most important things. Relationships with a spouse, children, family, friends, and colleagues are not easy and require a lifetime of continuous work. I wish I had been taught this earlier in life. For young people to navigate dealing well with others, positive interactions must be learned, valued, and appreciated. In academic spaces where this is not so, creating social awareness takes work and requires time and lots of patience. Nevertheless, teachers can start by integrating social awareness and reflection into project lessons.

Research suggests that students can simultaneously improve social interactions and academic achievement (B. Hurst et al., 2013). However, remember that social and emotional learning (SEL) strategies require consistent interventions before they stick (Hattie, 2009).

In a study by B. Hurst et al. (2013), students in three different ELA undergraduate and graduate courses reflected following every class period for a semester on the correlation between social interactions and their literacy skills. The results showed that participants felt that favorable social interactions positively impacted their knowledge of literacy and problem-solving skills (B. Hurst et al., 2013). With this premise, this chapter provides a project for helping learners understand how social-awareness skills can be used to connect meaningfully with others and boost their learning of academic content. Hopefully, the project and its lessons can jumpstart learners on a positive and fulfilling path of good relationship management and happier lives.

THE SOCIAL-AWARENESS PROJECT: IMPROVING OUR RELATIONSHIPS

Project Description

Young people can improve their social-awareness skills to create a thriving school community for each other and the adults they interact with daily. This project creates space and opportunity for learners to take on the role of change advocates and explore how they can understand other people's feelings and their points of view. They will build empathy, learning to appreciate and respect people different from them as well as learning to follow the rules for interacting appropriately in different social situations at school. They will also learn how to leverage the help from their family and school community by contributing to a class mural. The mural can be painted on a wall or section of the class or school. If painting is not possible, the mural can also be designed and displayed on a bulletin board using paper products. Aspects of this project can also be implemented as a performance task.

Project Duration and Grade Levels

- Approximately 5.5 weeks
- Grade Level: Middle to high school (6–12)
  - Teachers may need to apply the content standards that fit their content and grade level.

Driving Question (DQ)

- Since students are improving their own social awareness and in community with others, there will be two DQs for the project. For one DQ, they will answer independently, and for the other, they will answer with their classmates.
  1. *How do I improve my social-awareness skills to understand better how others feel and to see their point of view?*
  2. *How does our class, as part of the larger school community, create a mural representing each unique individual and how they can add value to others?*

Content Standards and SEL Connections

- **CCSS.ELA-Literacy.W.6–8.3:** Write narratives to develop real or imagined experiences or events using effective technique, well-chosen details, and well-structured event sequences.

- **CCSS.ELA-Literacy.W.6–8.3.d:** Use concrete words and phrases and sensory details to convey experiences and events precisely.

- **CCSS.ELA-Literacy.W.6–8.3.e:** Provide a conclusion that follows from and reflects on the narrated experiences or events.

- **CCSS.Math.Content.7.G.A.1:** Solve problems involving scale drawings of geometric figures, including computing actual lengths and areas from a scale drawing and reproducing a scale drawing at a different scale.

- **CCSS.Math.Content.7.RP.A.2:** Recognize and represent proportional relationships between quantities.

- **CCSS.Math.Content.MP.1:** Make sense of problems and persevere in solving them.

- **CCSS.Math.Content.MP.2:** Reason abstractly and quantitatively.

- **CCSS.Math.Content.MP.4:** Model with mathematics.

- **CCSS.Math.Content.MP.5:** Use appropriate tools strategically.

- **CCSS.Math.Content.MP.6:** Attend to precision.

- **CCSS.Math.Content.MP.7:** Look for and make use of structure.

The National Core Arts Standards (NCAS) that can also be used for creating a mural in visual arts class or other classes include the following strands:

1. **Creating:**
   - Conceive and develop new artistic ideas and work.
   - Organize and develop artistic ideas and work.

2. **Presenting:**
   - Interpret and share artistic work.
   - Convey meaning through the presentation of artistic work.

3. **Responding:**
   - Interpret intent and meaning in artistic work.
   - Apply criteria to evaluate artistic work.

4. **Connecting:**
   - Relate artistic ideas and work with personal meaning and external context.
   - Synthesize and relate knowledge and personal experiences to make art.
   - Relate artistic ideas and works with societal, cultural, and historical contexts to deepen understanding.

Students should demonstrate their understanding of the strands outlined on the previous page by developing the mural's concept and researching, planning, and creating the final product to effectively communicate their ideas of adding value to others. They should also reflect on their collective work and connect the ideas captured on their mural to their class and school community's broader cultural and social context. If the teacher implementing this portion of the project needs to gain more experience with visual arts, I recommend seeking an expert, such as an art teacher or local artist, to assist the class with both the mural design and implementation.

Learn more about the NCAS here: https://bit.ly/3YHbWlG

- **SEL Connection(s):** Social awareness includes empathy, understanding the feelings of others, respect, seeking assistance, cultural competence, active listening, teamwork, and seeking to help others.

- **Literacy Connection(s):** Reading and writing, analyzing and evaluating text, summarizing and synthesizing information. Writing clear and coherent sentences, using appropriate grammar, spelling, and punctuation. Developing ideas and supporting them with personal insight. Organizing and presenting a personal narrative using clear and concise language, organization, and reflection.

- **Numeracy Connection(s):** Measurement, using basic geometric shapes and principles to design mural, proportions, scaling, estimation and budgeting, and ensuring the mural is symmetrical and balanced.

Learning Intentions

1. I can write a 500-word personal narrative about my personal experience with empathy and how it impacted me and others at my school.

2. I can write clearly and concisely, referencing essential details of my experience with the benefits of empathy in my narrative.

3. I can use transitions to connect and organize my narrative with a clear start, middle, and conclusion.

4. I can reflect in my narrative on my experience with empathy and what I learned about the importance of social awareness for building community with others at my school.

5. I can identify a classmate or teacher for whom I will create an empathy map.

6. I can gather statements from my classmate or teacher that can provide insights into their needs.

7. I can identify and understand the thoughts and feelings that my classmate or teacher might have based their actions and words on.

8. I can identify the challenges that my classmate or teacher might face.

9. I can use the empathy map I created to develop more positive outcomes for my classmate or teacher.

10. I can determine the size of the surface where the mural will be designed and painted.

11. I can measure the different sections of the mural design to ensure accurate proportions and placement.

12. I can determine the materials needed for the mural, such as paint, brushes, and other supplies.

13. I can track expenses to ensure the project stays within the allotted budget.

14. I can use basic geometric shapes and principles like triangles, circles, and lines to create the mural design.

15. I can adjust the size of the mural design while maintaining proper proportions and visual appeal.

16. I can add my name and one word to the mural describing how I will add value to others in my class and school community.

17. I can use symmetry and balance to create visually appealing designs in the mural.

18. I can seal the mural to protect it from weather and other forms of damage.

19. I can select appropriate audience members who will benefit most from the information presented.

20. I can develop my artist statement and talk to be appropriate for my audience and explain the inspiration for the mural.

21. I can present information clearly and concisely using photographs or a time-lapse video to ensure the audience understands the mural design process.

22. I can use appropriate language and tone to engage my audience.

Final Products With Details

1. **Personal Narrative About Empathy**: Students compose an original personal narrative of about 500 words defining and detailing their experience with empathy and how it impacted them and others at their school. They may describe an event where empathy was shown to them or vice versa. The narrative should include individual students' reflections on their personal experiences with the benefits of empathy. The narrative should also provide the following:

   - Adherence to good grammar and sentence structure
   - Clear organization with a start, middle, and end
   - Takeaways on the importance of social awareness for building a positive and safe school community

2. **Empathy Map**: Students will create an empathy map as a helpful tool for being kind and connecting better with others by understanding better how they may feel. They may choose another classmate or a teacher as the subject of their map. To create their empathy map, students will observe what the other person says and does and then imagine themselves as that person and think about what they might think and feel.

3. **Mural Design and Public Unveiling**: Students will work with their teacher, classmates, and other adults to design a mural to showcase everyone in the class's name and one word to describe how they will add value to each other and the overall school community. They will complete these steps:

- Identify a wall or space to design the mural in their classroom or school. They can decide to either paint the mural or use paper products.

- Use basic geometric shapes and principles to create the mural design.

- Adjust the size of the mural design while maintaining proper proportions and visual appeal.

- Determine the materials needed for the mural and remain within a budget.

- Create a compelling artistic presentation using technology.

Phase 1: Compelling Hook and Initial Teacher Lessons

The compelling hook launches the project to engage learners. Learn more about the significance of the compelling hook in project-based learning (PBL) in Chapter 9 on page 107. To help provide a solid foundation for completing the personal narrative, the teacher facilitates a mini-lesson(s) on social awareness, showing empathy, and the essential components of a personal narrative. The students will compose their narratives in three drafts and receive a feedback cycle after each draft. Their narrative will help them build essential knowledge and frame their thoughts and beliefs on empathy's benefits on themselves, their classmates, and the larger school community. The personal narrative activity is also a scaffold for the following products in the project—the empathy map and mural design.

Phase 1: Instructional Alignment Tool

PRODUCT(S) AND TASKS	LEARNING INTENTIONS AND PACING	FORMAL AND INFORMAL FORMATIVE ASSESSMENTS	MINI-LESSONS, HIGH-YIELDING STRATEGIES, AND SCAFFOLDS
Personal Narrative (3–4 class periods)	I can write a 500-word personal narrative about my personal experience with empathy and how it impacted me and others at my school (3–4 class periods)	• Brainstorm ideas in graphic organizer • Personal narrative draft 1 • Responses during classroom discussions • Exit ticket	• Teacher-led mini-lesson explaining major concepts • Teacher modeling personal narrative • Graphic organizer to organize thoughts and ideas • All-class discussion and debrief

PRODUCT(S) AND TASKS	LEARNING INTENTIONS AND PACING	FORMAL AND INFORMAL FORMATIVE ASSESSMENTS	MINI-LESSONS, HIGH-YIELDING STRATEGIES, AND SCAFFOLDS
	I can write clearly and concisely, referencing essential details of my experience with the benefits of empathy in my narrative (3 class periods)	• Draft 1 Feedback protocol using rubric • Update graphic organizer • Reflect and revise • Exit ticket	• Teacher-led empathy-building activity • Graphic organizer • Teacher/student feedback • Whole-class reflection
	I can use transitions to connect and organize my narrative with a clear start, middle, and conclusion (3 class periods)	• Teacher-led discussion • Begin draft 2 • Feedback protocol using rubric • Update graphic organizer • Exit ticket	• Mini-lesson on transitions • Individual and small-group teaching • Graphic organizer • Teacher/student feedback
	I can reflect in my narrative on my experience with empathy and what I learned about the importance of social awareness for building community with others at my school (1 class period)	• Begin draft 3 • Update graphic organizer • Discussion with teacher • Exit ticket	• Individual and small-group teaching • Additional resources pertaining to grammar and sentence structure • Teacher/student feedback • Graphic organizer

Important Note: Teachers can develop their *Social Awareness* mini-lesson using the following resources.

PERSONAL NARRATIVE WRITING GUIDE	NARRATIVE WRITING GRAPHIC ORGANIZER	6 WAYS OF TEACHING EMPATHY TO KIDS IN THE CLASSROOM
https://bit.ly/41dBr6r	https://bit.ly/3xBAyXL	https://bit.ly/3l6vHTq

Phase 2: Complete an Empathy Map

With a better understanding of the importance of social awareness by understanding how others may feel, the students will create an empathy map for someone. The empathy map template can be found in Chapter 3, page 36, and the companion website to this book. They can choose either a peer or a teacher for the activity. The teacher provides a template with the following four quadrants:

1. What I heard ___ said.

2. What I saw ___ do.

3. What I think ___ thinks.

4. What I think ___ feels.

Using Post-It notes or free-handing on each quadrant, the learners will pay close attention to what their subject says and does. The **What I heard** quadrant should have actual quotes from the participant. For example, a peer may say, "I like to complete my work by myself." A teacher may say, "I love teaching, but it's difficult when some students talk and disrupt my lesson." By paying close attention to behavior and actions, the learners should state only what they saw done in the **What I saw** quadrant. Doing so will give them context for what they believe the person thinks and feels. Once an empathy map is completed, the students will better understand how the person feels and why they do what they do. This newly developed insight can be used to make better connections and rapport with others within the class and wider school community. Teachers should facilitate a mini-lesson and provide a completed example of an empathy map.

PRODUCT(S) AND TASKS	LEARNING INTENTIONS AND PACING	FORMAL AND INFORMAL FORMATIVE ASSESSMENTS	MINI-LESSONS, HIGH-YIELDING STRATEGIES, AND SCAFFOLDS
Empathy Map (3 class periods)	I can Identify my classmate or teacher for whom I will create an empathy map (1 class period)	• Brainstorm ideas • Begin developing empathy map • Responses during classroom discussions • Exit ticket	• Teacher-led mini-lesson explaining major concepts • Teacher modeling empathy map development • Empathy map template • All-class discussion and debrief
	I can gather statements from my classmate or teacher that can provide insights into their needs (2 class periods)	• Feedback protocol using rubric • Update empathy map • Reflect and revise • Exit ticket	• Teacher-led empathy-building activity • Empathy map template • Teacher/student feedback • Whole-class reflection
	I can identify and understand the thoughts and feelings that my classmate or teacher might have based on their actions and words (2 class periods)	• Teacher-led discussion • Update empathy map • Reflect and revise • Exit ticket	• Mini-lesson on empathy • Individual and small-group teaching • Empathy map template • Teacher/student feedback
	I can identify the challenges that my classmate or teacher might face (1 class period)	• Update empathy map • Feedback protocol using rubric • Discussion with teacher • Exit ticket	• Individual and small-group teaching • Additional resources pertaining to using empathy maps • Empathy map template • Teacher/student feedback

(Continued)

(Continued)

PRODUCT(S) AND TASKS	LEARNING INTENTIONS AND PACING	FORMAL AND INFORMAL FORMATIVE ASSESSMENTS	MINI-LESSONS, HIGH-YIELDING STRATEGIES, AND SCAFFOLDS
	I can use the empathy map I created to develop more positive outcomes for my classmate or teacher (1 class period)	• Personal reflection • Responses during classroom discussions • Exit ticket	• Individual and small-group teaching • Additional resources pertaining to using empathy maps • Empathy map template • Teacher/student feedback

Important Note: Teachers can develop their *framework or model for building empathy* using the following resources.

LESSON RESOURCES

HOW TO USE AN EMPATHY MAP FOR RELATIONSHIP BUILDING

https://bit.ly/3ElrqKy

EMPATHY MAP TEMPLATE

https://bit.ly/3ICf03C

Phase 3: Mural Design and Public Unveiling

The mural design may take 1.5 to 3 weeks to complete—especially if it's being painted. If it's your first time designing a mural, be flexible on its development timeline and seek expert assistance. Have your learners be intentional about the wall or space to showcase the mural and use geometric shapes in its design while maintaining proper proportions and visual appeal. Help them determine the materials needed for the mural and the budget. Before the public unveiling, students should consider, plan, and rehearse the steps they'll take to present the mural to the community.

Like artists, the class may prepare an artist's statement and talk explaining the mural's purpose, inspiration, and contribution to the school community. The students may also use photographs or a time-lapse video showcasing the process from start to finish. During the unveiling, students will engage with the public and guide them through the concepts and content of the mural while answering questions that elucidate their ideas. After they present, students should reflect with their teacher to discuss their growth and challenges and set goals for future projects.

Phase 3: Instructional Alignment Tool

PRODUCT(S) AND TASKS	LEARNING INTENTIONS AND PACING	FORMAL AND INFORMAL FORMATIVE ASSESSMENTS	MINI-LESSONS, HIGH-YIELDING STRATEGIES, AND SCAFFOLDS
Mural Design **(7–8 class periods)**	• I can determine the size of the surface where the mural will be designed and painted. • I can measure the different sections of the mural design to ensure accurate proportions and placement. (2–3 class periods)	• Brainstorm ideas and sketch the design • Space measurement • Responses during classroom discussions • Exit ticket	• Teacher-led mini-lesson on measurement, proportions, and placement for mural • Teacher modeling • All-class discussion and debrief
	• I can determine the materials needed for the mural, such as paint, brushes, and other supplies. • I can track expenses to ensure the project stays within the allotted budget. (1 class period)	• Materials list development and checklist • Updating budget spreadsheet • Responses during classroom discussions • Exit ticket	• Teacher-led mini-lesson on materials and budgeting • Budget spreadsheet template • Teacher/student feedback • Whole-class reflection

(Continued)

(Continued)

PRODUCT(S) AND TASKS	LEARNING INTENTIONS AND PACING	FORMAL AND INFORMAL FORMATIVE ASSESSMENTS	MINI-LESSONS, HIGH-YIELDING STRATEGIES, AND SCAFFOLDS
	• I can use basic geometric shapes and principles like triangles, circles, and lines to create the mural design. • I can adjust the size of the mural design while maintaining proper proportions and visual appeal. (3–4 class periods)	• Sketch the details using geometric shapes • Check for proper proportions and visual appeal • Reflect and revise • Exit ticket	• Mini-lesson on using geometric shapes in art • Individual and small-group teaching • Critique with an expert (proper proportions and visual appeal) • Teacher/student feedback
	• I can add my name and one word to the mural describing how I will add value to others in my class and school community. • I can use symmetry and balance to create visually appealing designs in the mural. • I can seal the mural to protect it from weather and other forms of damage. (5–6 class periods)	• Sketch and paint the details • Reflect and revise • Add finishing touches • Seal the mural • Exit ticket	• Teacher-led mini-lesson on symmetry and balance • Individual and small-group teaching • Critique with an expert empathy map template • Teacher/student feedback

PRODUCT(S) AND TASKS	LEARNING INTENTIONS AND PACING	FORMAL AND INFORMAL FORMATIVE ASSESSMENTS	MINI-LESSONS, HIGH-YIELDING STRATEGIES, AND SCAFFOLDS
Public Unveiling (2–3 class periods)	I can select appropriate audience members who will benefit most from the information presented (1 class period)	• Written notes and reflection • Responses during classroom discussions • Exit ticket	• Teacher-led mini-lesson explaining major concepts • Videos showcasing presentations • All-class discussion and debrief
	I can develop my artist statement and talk to be appropriate for my audience and explain the inspiration for the mural (2–3 class periods)	• Feedback protocol using rubric • Presentation checklist • Exit ticket	• Teacher directions and guiding questions • Presentation app (e.g., PowerPoint) • Teacher/student feedback
	I can present information clearly and concisely using photographs or a time-lapse video to ensure the audience understands the mural design process (2–3 class periods)	• Teacher-led discussion • Time-lapse video editing • Photo journal development • Feedback protocol using rubric • Checklist • Exit ticket	• Individual and small-group rehearsal • Additional resources pertaining to presentations • Presentation app • Teacher/student feedback
	I can use appropriate language and tone in my presentation to engage my audience (3 class periods)	• Written notes • Discussion with teacher	• Individual and small-group rehearsal • Additional resources pertaining to specific expert(s) • Teacher/student feedback

HOW TO CREATE A SUCCESSFUL MURAL WITH YOUNGER STUDENTS

https://bit.ly/416XsUt

12 KEY STEPS TO LEADING AMAZING MURAL PROJECTS

https://bit.ly/3EnrARX

MURAL DESIGN BUDGET TEMPLATE

https://bit.ly/413x65X

BASIC MURAL SUPPLIES

https://bit.ly/3IS5osw

BRINGING IDENTITY WORK TO PBL VIDEO

https://edut.to/3IDRZUT

HOW TO ORGANIZE AN ART EXHIBITION

https://bit.ly/3xyyUGq

Important Note: In addition to using the resources above, teachers can develop their facilitation skills and have students use the single-point rubrics by accessing the full Passion to Purpose PBL+ Project Template in Appendix A.

CHAPTER 8

....

RESPONSIBLE DECISION MAKING

From Awareness to Action

Students make decisions every day, though not always the best ones. Teachers can use social and emotional learning (SEL) to help them make responsible and better ones. When young people learn responsible decision making, they are better equipped to navigate the challenges and complexities of life, such as improving their safety and well-being, success at school, and avoiding peer pressure (Eisenberg et al., 2010). With some students reporting dissatisfactions with school, such as peer pressure, feeling unsafe, and wanting more self-agency (National Center for Education Statistics, 2021), responsible decision making is an important SEL competency for them to improve alongside adults. The National Association of Secondary School Principals (2022) reported the following:

- Seventy-four percent of students reported they needed help with their mental or emotional health last school year.

- Fifty-one percent of students reported they had been threatened or attacked verbally or physically during the past school year. Seventy percent of school leaders also reported the same.

- Seventy-three percent of students reported they were typically satisfied at their school but would like more opportunities to be involved in the development of school policies and planning.

- Both school leaders and students reported that more work needs to be done to meet the needs of underserved students.

As we can see, assisting students with developing decision-making skills is imperative when learners are young. Later, these skills can serve them well in their careers and relationships.

THE ROLE OF THE BRAIN IN DECISION MAKING

In my work in schools and with students, I have witnessed young people behaving impulsively and appearing to lack good decision-making skills. It can be highly stressful for the teachers and other adults needing to intervene, help, and teach them better ways of problem solving—especially when it's recurring. At times, adults are perplexed at the decisions some of their students make, but often they don't understand the science of decision making or the role of the brain in the process. This is critical information to know and comprehend when attempting to help kids make better choices.

Responsible decision making requires high levels of cognition and is tied to the prefrontal cortex—the brain's rational part that's responsible for executive functions (Fisher, 2018). This part of the brain is needed for planning, making sound judgments, controlling impulses, and making good decisions. The prefrontal cortex develops throughout adolescence to age 25 (Campellone & Turley, 2021). Young people, teens, and adults who have not learned responsible decision making tend to respond impulsively from the emotional part of the brain—the amygdala (Valenzuela, 2021e). Getting them started learning responsible decision making during this development stage is critical. PBL+ can provide students with frequent opportunities to practice their decision-making skills by engaging them in collaboration, communication, reflection, self-assessment, feedback, and evaluation.

THE RESPONSIBLE DECISION-MAKING PROJECT

Spreading Awareness Through Campaigns

Learning to make responsible decisions is important for teenagers' personal development and lifelong learning. In this project, students will develop awareness about the science of decision making and learn to use tools that help them evaluate their options using well-thought-out processes involving various age-appropriate scenarios. They will hone their decision-making skills through role-play, class discussions, and the creation of an impactful campaign with a call to action to raise awareness about issues affecting students at their school. To fully develop their campaigns, they will work in teams to choose and understand a topic, develop a call to action, identify a target audience, and create engaging content to deliver their message effectively and publicly.

Project Duration and Grade Levels

- Approximately 3.5 weeks
- Grade Level: Middle to high school (6–12)
  - Teachers may need to apply the content standards that fit their content and grade level.

Driving Question (DQ)

- Since students are improving their own decision-making skills and in community with others, there will be two DQs for the project. For one DQ, they will answer independently; for the other, they will respond with their classmates.

1. *How do I improve my responsible decision-making skills to create better outcomes for both myself and others?*

2. *How can we, as _____, create a campaign to raise awareness about _____ in order to improve _____ for _____ in our school community?* (e.g., "How can we, as <u>advocates</u>, create a campaign to raise awareness about <u>campus bullying</u> in order to improve <u>safety</u> for <u>all</u> in our school community?")

> **Important Note for Teachers:** A campaign is an organized course of action to achieve a goal. In the adult world, campaigns are created by various people and organizations, such as activists and advocates, political parties and candidates, business and nonprofit organizations, and government agencies. Allow students to select a role they want to assume as campaign creators.

Content Standards and SEL Connections

- **CCSS.ELA-Literacy.W.9-10.1.B:** Develop claim(s) and counterclaims fairly, supplying evidence for each while pointing out the strengths and limitations of both in a manner that anticipates the audience's knowledge level and concerns.

- **CCSS.ELA-Literacy.SL.9-10.4:** Present information, findings, and supporting evidence clearly, concisely, and logically such that listeners can follow the line of reasoning and the organization, development, substance, and style are appropriate to purpose, audience, and task.

- **CCSS.ELA-Literacy.RI.9-10.7:** Analyze various accounts of a subject told in different mediums (e.g., a person's life story in both print and multimedia), determining which details are emphasized in each account.

- **CCSS.ELA-Literacy.W.9-10.6:** Use technology, including the internet, to produce, publish, and update individual or shared writing products, taking advantage of technology's capacity to link to other information and to display information flexibly and dynamically.

- **CCSS.Math.Content.HSA.SSE.A.1.a:** Interpret parts of an expression, such as terms, factors, and coefficients.

- **CCSS.Math.Content.6.SP.A.1:** Recognize a statistical question as one that anticipates variability in the data related to the question and accounts for it in the answers.

- **CCSS.Math.Content.7.SP.A.2:** Use data from a random sample to draw inferences about a population with an unknown characteristic of interest. Generate multiple samples (or simulated samples) of the same size to gauge the variation in estimates or predictions.

As campaign creators, students should demonstrate their understanding of the aforementioned standards by understanding the issue they're raising awareness about, developing a clear message and call to action, identifying a target audience, collaborating with others to create engaging content and planning, and executing their campaign. They should also reflect on ways to improve their collective work and connect the ideas in their respective campaigns to improve the school climate by teaching others about the importance of responsible decision making.

Learn more about the components of creating campaigns here: https://bit.ly/ 3KChW1O

If the teacher implementing this portion of the project needs to gain more experience with campaign creation, I recommend seeking an expert to assist the class with the campaign creation and implementation.

- **SEL Connection(s):** Responsible decision making includes identifying and analyzing choices and options, considering multiple perspectives, goal setting and planning, recognizing solutions that benefit all parties, and reflection and evaluation.

- **Literacy Connection(s):** Reading and writing, analyzing and evaluating text, summarizing and synthesizing information. Developing claims and counterclaims. Clear communication, analyzing multiple perspectives, and technological literacy.

- **Numeracy Connection(s):** Interpretation of mathematical expressions, identifying statistical questions and inference, and sampling.

Learning Intentions

1. I can complete a decision-making matrix to help me analyze multiple choices with possible outcomes.

2. I can identify two to three possible decisions for a given situation.

3. I can weigh each decision's pros and cons to determine the most responsible choice.

4. I can add and subtract positive and negative numbers using a number line.

5. I can make thoughtful and informed decisions based on the information I have gathered and analyzed.

6. I can communicate my decision and explain my rationale for making it to others.

7. I can survey my classmates and school community members to decide on a significant issue that will be addressed in my campaign.

8. I can understand the issue I am raising awareness about for my campaign.

9. I can develop a clear message and call to action for my campaign.

10. I can connect the ideas in my campaign to the goal of improving responsible decision making in my school community.

11. I can collaborate with others to create and present engaging content for my campaign.

12. I can identify a target audience for my campaign.

13. I can use my campaign to teach others the importance of responsible decision making to improve the school climate and culture.

Final Products With Details

1. **Responsible Decision-Making Matrix:** Students will complete a decision-making matrix to help them make better decisions between up to three choices by weighing options and evaluating the impact (pros and cons) on themselves and others using a simple point system, with positive numbers for pros and negative ones for cons. After tallying their numbers, the decision with the highest score can be deemed the most responsible one.

2. **Awareness Campaign:** Students will collaborate with peers and adults to create an awareness campaign about an issue affecting school community members. They will do the following:

   • Explore the issue they're raising awareness about inside and out.

   • Develop a clear message and call to action.

   • Identify a target audience.

   • Create engaging content such as public service announcements, roleplays, ads, articles, and podcasts.

   • Connect the ideas in their campaigns to improve the school climate by teaching others about the importance of responsible decision making.

Phase 1: Compelling Hook and Initial Teacher Lessons

The compelling hook launches the project to engage learners. Learn more about the significance of the compelling hook in project-based learning (PBL) in Chapter 9 on page 107. To help provide a solid foundation for completing the responsible decision making matrix (tool), the teacher facilitates a mini-lesson(s) on the science and the role of the brain in decision making and models how to use the tool to evaluate their decisions. The students will complete the tool and receive feedback upon completion. Each student will have the opportunity to explain their decision and rationale for making it in written or oral form—depending on time, they may do both. The decision-making process afforded by the tool is a scaffold for the awareness campaign they will design in the project's second phase.

Phase 1: Instructional Alignment Tool

PRODUCT(S) AND TASKS	LEARNING INTENTIONS AND PACING	FORMAL AND INFORMAL FORMATIVE ASSESSMENTS	MINI-LESSONS, HIGH-YIELDING STRATEGIES, AND SCAFFOLDS
Responsible Decision-Making Matrix **(2 class periods)**	I can complete a decision-making matrix to help me analyze multiple choices with possible outcomes. (2 class periods)	• Brainstorm ideas • Begin developing the responsible decision-making matrix • Responses during classroom discussions • Exit ticket	• Teacher-led mini-lesson explaining major concepts • Teacher modeling use of the decision-making matrix • Responsible decision-making template • All-class discussion and debrief
	• I can identify two to three possible decisions for a given situation. • I can weigh each decision's pros and cons to determine the most responsible choice. • I can add and subtract positive and negative numbers using a number line. (1 class period)	• Teacher-led discussion • Update responsible decision-making matrix • Reflect and revise • Exit ticket	• Teacher modeling decision making and relevant math skills • Individual and small-group teaching • Responsible decision-making template • Teacher/student feedback • Whole-class reflection
	• I can make thoughtful and informed decisions based on the information I have gathered and analyzed. • I can communicate my decision and explain my rationale for making it to others. (1 class period)	• Update responsible decision-making matrix • Feedback protocol using rubric • Discussion with teacher • Exit ticket	• Individual and small-group teaching • Additional resources pertaining to using the responsible decision-making matrix • Responsible decision-making template • Teacher/student feedback • Whole-class reflection

LESSON RESOURCES

A TOOL TO HELP STUDENTS MAKE GOOD DECISIONS

https://edut.to/3KMIGxD

DECISION-MAKING LESSONS AND SCENARIOS

https://bit.ly/3m4e9Qn

RESPONSIBLE DECISION-MAKING MATRIX TEMPLATE

https://bit.ly/3SBdz93

HOW TO ADD AND SUBTRACT POSITIVE & NEGATIVE NUMBERS LESSON

https://bit.ly/2EJUTkC

Phase 2: Awareness Campaign

The awareness campaign will take time and may take 2 to 3.5 weeks to complete. If it's your first time coaching students through developing campaigns, be flexible on its development timeline and seek expert assistance. Be sure to provide lessons, frequent modeling, and examples of various issues they can explore and successful campaigns. Chances are some of your students are already using media to create videos, sound bites, and podcasts—have them apply that knowledge to the campaign they create. Ask them to brainstorm issues they select and encourage them to explore the problem fully.

Like professional campaign creators, the students will prepare a call to action (CTA) to encourage the school community to get involved in the campaign's objective. The students may also use photographs and short videos to showcase the process from start to finish on the school's or class's social media accounts. While implementing their campaigns, students will engage with the public and guide them through their campaigns' essential concepts and CTA while answering questions. After they present, students should reflect with their teacher to discuss their growth and challenges and set goals for future projects.

PRODUCT(S) AND TASKS	LEARNING INTENTIONS AND PACING	FORMAL AND INFORMAL FORMATIVE ASSESSMENTS	MINI-LESSONS, HIGH-YIELDING STRATEGIES, AND SCAFFOLDS
Awareness Campaign (6–8 class periods)	• I can survey my classmates and school community members to decide on a significant issue that will be addressed in my campaign. • I can understand the issue I am raising awareness about for my campaign. (2–3 class periods)	• Explore issues that need solving in the school community • Create survey in Google Forms • Responses during classroom discussions • Exit ticket	• Teacher-led mini-lesson on campaigns and surveying • Teacher modeling • Teacher-curated resources on issues for students to explore • All-class discussion and debrief
	• I can develop a clear message and call to action for my campaign. • I can connect the ideas in my campaign to the goal of improving responsible decision making in my school community. (2 class periods)	• Call to action development • Using and reviewing the responsible decision-making matrix • Responses during classroom discussions • Exit ticket	• Teacher-led mini-lesson on developing calls to action • Responsible decision-making matrix template • Teacher/student feedback • Whole-class reflection
	• I can collaborate with others to create and present engaging content for my campaign.	• Using media and edtech tools • Brainstorming appropriate audience	• Individual and small-group teaching on various edtech and media tools (may be led by experts) • Critique with an expert

PRODUCT(S) AND TASKS	LEARNING INTENTIONS AND PACING	FORMAL AND INFORMAL FORMATIVE ASSESSMENTS	MINI-LESSONS, HIGH-YIELDING STRATEGIES, AND SCAFFOLDS
	• I can identify a target audience for my campaign. (3–4 class periods)	• Reflect and revise • Exit ticket	• Teacher directions and guiding questions • Teacher/student feedback
	• I can use my campaign to teach others the importance of responsible decision making to improve the school climate and culture. (After the project)	• Making the work available to the public (intended audience) • Reflect and revise • Add finishing touches • Exit ticket	• Teacher-led mini-lesson on implementing campaigns • Individual and small-group teaching • Critique with an expert • Teacher/student feedback

LESSON RESOURCES

FIRE UP YOUR STUDENTS WITH A CAMPAIGN PROJECT

https://bit.ly/3Yge6yg

8 STEPS TO CREATING A SOCIAL MEDIA CAMPAIGN

https://bit.ly/3kHtGW4

CAMPAIGN TOPICS AND EXAMPLES

https://bit.ly/3ml9Pwo

Important Note: Teachers can develop their facilitation skills and have students use single-point rubrics by accessing the full Passion to Purpose PBL+ Project Template in Appendix A.

PART 3

....

A ROADMAP TO STUDENT ENGAGEMENT AND RIGOROUS PBL

The following chapters provide readers with a clear road map and strategies for engaging students and maintaining academic rigor in project-based learning (PBL). In it, I offer concrete steps to student engagement, collaboration with others (adults and peers), social and emotional learning (SEL), preparing students for the public product, and tools for managing complex components of a project. The tools and practices in these chapters are designed to refine your PBL teaching plan using adaptable high-yielding strategies that engage and compel learners to do their best work. For continuity, readers will find connections in these chapters to the elements uplifted in the PBL+ framework from the first section and the adaptable SEL-infused projects provided in the second section.

CHAPTER 9

....

USING A 5-STEP ROADMAP TO ACTIVATE STUDENT ENGAGEMENT AND RIGOROUS PBL

This chapter is all about engaging students from the start to the end of projects and performance tasks using three simple engagement strategies and five calculated steps. These five steps will hook students at the start of projects and keep them engaged till the end. The corresponding PBL+ Special Interest Project Planner can be used to keep track of their work and reflect at every step.

I recently added the following three engagement strategies to my daily teaching and coaching because of the current state of teaching. The last few years have shown me that teachers need to engage students in their classes more than ever—having a system and go-to strategies they can rely on can make a difference in many classrooms. My hope is that you are able to balance the advice in this chapter along with the elements of the PBL+ Framework outlined in Part 1 of this book. Student engagement is vital for a successful project and school year.

STUDENT ENGAGEMENT IS THE FIRST STEP TO RIGOROUS PBL

Education writers at Harvard Business Publishing (2022) explain that declining student engagement is one of teachers' most significant challenges in post-pandemic teaching. Therefore, we must consider student engagement when designing and facilitating our project and performance task units. Unfortunately, teacher professional development doesn't always help teachers plan for student engagement. Before planning for engagement, let's learn why it matters.

Across grade levels and multiple disciplines, academic research supports a strong correlation between student engagement and student achievement (Dyer, 2015). Academic engagement is often defined as students actively participating by focusing on a task or activity. In *Visible Learning*, researcher John Hattie (2009) explains that schools will only successfully implement new academic initiatives if they face and resolve student engagement first. This is why student engagement sets the path toward rigorous project-based learning (PBL) in this chapter.

As part of my coaching work, I'm often requested to model with students the teaching strategies we want teachers to adapt in their own practice. Unfortunately, I have seen high levels of apathy and disengagement in youth that prevent them from meaningful learning. In our sessions, colleagues frequently ask me, "How do we engage younger kids who don't want to be here or do their work?" The truth is that it's deeper than selecting and adapting a set of high-yielding engagement strategies in cases where disengagement exists. In these situations, individual teachers and teaching teams may need to first consider the following questions:

1. *Can I precisely identify the reasons why my students are disengaged and categorize those that are within my control and those that are not?* This requires us to survey students and take stock of our classroom setting. Every teacher knows the distractions we can fix and those that need administrative assistance and wraparound services for more challenging student behaviors.

   Wraparound services comprise comprehensive and holistic care for students and their families experiencing mental health or behavioral challenges (Valenzuela, 2022e). Wraparound programs that provide these services are typically collaborations between state or local government agencies and organizations working in schools (Colburn & Beggs, 2021).

2. *What factors are proven to significantly influence students' engagement in the grade band I teach?* For example, factors that impact student engagement may include communication, collaboration, positive interactions, and timely feedback (DeVito, 2016)—strategies that I incorporate in this book.

   I recommend monitoring how your students respond to how you specifically implement these strategies—particularly the ones for engagement detailed in this chapter.

3. *What strategies support the factors that foster engagement, and how can I tweak and adapt them for my students?* Visible Learning strategies are an excellent place to start because Hattie (2009) uses the statistical measure of effect size to compare the impacts of various influences on academic achievement—including engagement.

   Effect size is a statistical concept measuring the strength of the relationship between two variables on a numeric scale (Complete Dissertation, n.d.). Hattie's meta-meta-study promotes schools adapting strategies with an effect size of 0.4 or better, as those have shown the power to create change in the impact of learning. For example, strategies <0.3 have a small impact, 0.4 have a medium impact, and >0.6 have a high impact (Hattie, 2009). In this book, I have selected and modeled only strategies with effect sizes of 0.4 or better.

What follows are three simple, but powerful and customizable, strategies for you to adapt to your classroom—even when you are not implementing projects.

THREE SIMPLE ENGAGEMENT STRATEGIES

1. Open Your Mail

I learned how to facilitate this activity from instructional designer Morgan Vien during a deeper learning workshop in Oakland, California, and it has stuck with me since. Open your mail is similar to a wellness check, except it focuses on learning needs instead of how someone feels. It's about getting students to open up to the teacher and one another. Teachers actively trying to create learning partnerships with students can use it to build engagement and empathy in the classroom. It also helps better engage kids who don't typically express what they need to learn.

Use the strategy at the start of the instructional day or learning block as an opportunity for students who would like to explain to their teachers and peers in a safe space what they need for the block of work time to be effective.

Here's how:

- Have your students circle up, standing for about 3–4 minutes, but they can also remain at their desks if space is an issue.

- Everyone doesn't have to talk, but everyone participates by paying attention to those expressing their learning needs.

- For younger kids, I recommend that teachers use sentence stems (e.g., "For me to learn this morning, I need my teacher to _____ and my classmates to _____").

Close the activity in an affirming tone that you have heard their needs and will do your best to keep the learning engaging.

2. Create Positive Vibes

I also learned to facilitate *create positive vibes* from Morgan Vein—it's always a hit with both youth and adults. This is an activity that I do to engage kids using movement in a fun, quick manner whenever I notice low energy for learning. I typically do it in a standing circle, which takes only 3–4 minutes. Again, we don't have to circle up every time—students can do this activity at their desks.

Teachers should explain that the purpose of the activity is to engage students and prepare them for learning whenever they need a pick-me-up. They should also teach students about the power of endorphins and how to create their own whenever they feel their energy fading. Endorphins are natural chemicals produced in the human body resulting from movement, laughter, and excitement (Fort Bend Taekwondo, 2019). I like to call them the body's natural antidepressant.

Teachers can be creative in how they help kids move (jumping jacks, a stretch, running in place, smiling, walking over to a peer to greet them, etc.). I like to toss an imaginary ball with my learners. Some choose to throw it, kick it, toss it, and so on. It always goes well and reengages kids. You'll want to close the activity by reaffirming its purpose of creating positive vibes.

3. Engage Kids Using Relevant Question Prompts

Good question prompts are great for helping learners to engage by getting to know each other better and with safe parameters. They can also be an excellent formative assessment, especially when question prompts call for learners to explain a personal connection to the content. I created the following question prompts for a sample environmental science PBL unit.

- What is the importance of caring for the environment?

- What kind of pollution personally bothers you most?

- Do you recycle? If so, what kinds of things do you recycle?

- Do you believe human activities contribute to climate change? If so, what should we do about it? If not, what do you think causes climate change?

- What overlap or connection do you see between social issues and environmental problems?

- Where do you go to breathe fresh air?

To make the activity fun, I use an interactive wheel and have students pair up for about 3 minutes, reminding them to share the airspace. Teachers can edit questions on the wheel based on their lesson context and the ages of learners.

To view the interactive wheel, please visit https://bit.ly/3hHJTJ6.

Here are a few question prompts I use to guide learner reflections and activate their prior knowledge for getting to know them and making authentic connections:

- What is your favorite book and why?

- Describe the attributes of a person you really admire.

- Talk about an object that is special to you. What makes it so special?

- How do you spend your free time?

- What is your favorite school subject, and how did it become your favorite?

- How do you use math strategies to solve problems at home?

Remember, creating engagement is both science and art. The former we can glean and adapt from the learning sciences, but the latter is our own personal style and the way we do things. Coupling them can make all the difference that our kids need to prepare for learning. Now that we have a few reliable engagement strategies, let's explore a five-step process to maintaining engagement and rigor throughout the entire process.

5 Steps to Rigorous PBL

As a PBL teacher and coach, I'm always looking for more efficient and effective ways to keep my learners compellingly engaged with the content from the start to the end of projects and performance tasks. There's no secret that sparking and sustaining engagement is a major concern for many educators in the post-COVID era (Harvard Business Publishing, 2022). The tricky part for many is twofold: first, designing a project that allows every kid in the class to see their interests reflected in the curriculum and, second, implementing a straightforward process every kid can see clearly to navigate. That's why I encourage teachers in my project ideation sessions to make space for at least one or two interest projects allowing kids to dive deeply into a topic of their choosing—but with the caveat that they engage in a five-step process designed to balance rigor with engagement.

We all know our students don't always think alike or share the same interests. Maybe the most common ground is that they all care about something—hopefully enough to work toward finding a solution for that very thing. For example, students concerned with their local environment may be compelled to engage in work that explores the causes of a problem and work with others to conjure up data-informed solutions (e.g., land restoration, forest restoration, habitat conservation). Similarly, kids who care about gaming, music, the arts, social media, or a social cause can engage through a process that propels them toward making conditions better for themselves and others. Some examples of topics kids may be interested in can include, but are not limited to, artificial intelligence in gaming, songwriting development, drawing vs. sketching, US infrastructure, or criminal justice reform.

Some teachers may feel lukewarm toward some of these topics and question how they align with what they teach. Remember, this is about garnering student interest and engaging them in a process we can leverage now for engagement and future work (the content we teach). I recommend implementing this type of special interest project once a semester and for only two to three weeks tops. What follows is the five-step engagement process you can use as a road map with special interest projects and other project types. Additionally, I recommend using the PBL+ Special Interest Project Planner on page 112 to allow students to reflect and document their work as they move through each step (see Figure 9.2).

Step 1: Begin With a Compelling Hook

A compelling hook is crucial for sparking student interest and engagement at the launch of projects and performance tasks. Also referred to as an entry event (Magnify Learning, n.d.), compelling hooks must be well planned to produce the following deliverables:

1. **Connection(s) between students and the work they'll be doing.** The more personalized your project theme is to your learners, the easier it is to build connections. Introducing a dynamic guest speaker, impact data, statistics, and exploration of their interest topic serve well for this purpose.

Team formation for partnering learners shouldn't be rushed, so I recommend you schedule at least two class periods for the compelling hook.

To be very deliberate in an interest project, survey your students prior and prepare a gallery walk for them to explore, showcasing compelling infographics that depict problems in their chosen topics. For example, if a student chooses habitat conversation as an interest, infographics displaying pollution and disruption of ecosystem processes can be highly compelling. Also, let's say a student says gaming is their interest—introducing the concept of adaptive gaming experiences (Eric, 2022) may very well compel them to create a solution(s) for improving gaming for users with disabilities.

To help students learn more about their interests, I created a curated document of PBL+ Resources for Special Interests and Passion Projects (https://bit.ly/3EPGOOS).

2. **Unpack the driving question (DQ).** As discussed in Chapter 4 on page 49, the DQ reminds students about what they aim to achieve as they work through the project and articulates the purpose of the project. During the compelling hook, teachers should spend some time helping students unpack what the DQ means and what they're aiming to accomplish by answering it. Essential vocabulary should be encapsulated in the DQ. If a term comes up repeatedly, include it in your DQ. Here are some DQ examples:

- How do we, as AI specialists, develop an AI-powered solution addressing the unique need of a client?

- How can we reduce our collective impact on our local watershed?

- How can we use multimedia effectively to demonstrate the role of photosynthesis in plant health?

In interest projects, student focuses will not be universal. They should therefore assist with composing their own DQs. Teacher-developed DQ starters can be the scaffold they need (see Figure 9.1).

FIGURE 9.1   TWO SAMPLE TEACHER-DEVELOPED DQ STARTERS

TEACHER-DEVELOPED DQ STARTER	STUDENTS FILL IN THE BLANKS WITH THEIR INTEREST
How do we, as _____, create _____ about _____?	How do we, as _conservationists_, create _awareness within our community_ about _protecting our trees_?
How can we, as _____, design _____ to _____?	How can we, as _physical trainers_, design _fitness regimens_ to meet _the unique needs of two clients_?

3. **Create a set of student-generated questions.** Typically, teachers develop sets of essential questions for students to answer in their unit plans—in PBL, the kids create a list of questions they want to answer by examining artifacts such as infographics, the DQ, and rubrics. They can record their questions in journals, chart papers, or Google Docs. This list is regarded as a living inventory of questions that ultimately must be answered to answer the DQ. Student-generated questions may look like the following:

- How does artificial intelligence impact various industries?

- What is the local watershed and why is it important to me?

- How does photosynthesis affect plants?

4. **Teams formation.** Team assignments need to be carried out with structure and purpose to set students up for successful collaboration. I like to implement the following activities in four steps (Valenzuela, 2019a):

- The Ideal Teammate Activity

- Setting Roles for Each Team Member

- First Team Meeting: Create Shared Agreements

- Team-Building Activities and Collaboration Measures

Effective team formation is such an important topic in PBL that I dedicated an entire chapter to it. These four steps are explained in full detail in Chapter 10 of this book.

5. **Critical documents curation (team contracts, task lists, rubrics, etc.).** Every project and performance task has several documents critical to the intended learning and must be curated and stored for easy access. I currently use Google Classroom and Canvas as the designated go-to for students to retrieve their docs. Teachers can use their school's learning management system (LMS) to do the same. Documents common to projects and performance tasks may include, but are not limited to, the following:

- An info sheet listing learning intentions, explaining the purpose of the project, providing the DQ, and the products students will be working on

- Rubrics

- Graphic organizers

- Tasks list

- Presentation scripts

- Academic one-pagers

Initially, some of these activities will be clunky—especially if it's the first time you or the students are attempting them. Don't be discouraged or lose trust in the process. Lead with grace, empathy, and transparency. Ask your learners to do the same as you try to compel them to engage in the work. Remember, thriving classrooms are co-created—teachers can't and shouldn't do it alone.

Step 2: Explore Major Concept(s)

In this step, students must be clear about the concept(s) within the chosen topic they'll be exploring—it helps when they're interested and compelled by the subject matter and the exploration steps are outlined for them. Another important note that I think teachers must convey to students is that exploration in this context means investigating a topic and learning about problems that need solving. Students will work on creating a solution(s) to at least one of those problems later in step 4 of this process. For instance, kids learning about the relationship between photosynthesis and plant health may discover that the school garden needs its soil tested. Further exploration and learning from a professional(s) may lead them to learn of the need to add compost to compact soil to increase plant air, water, and nutrients. Here's a three-step straightforward exploration process kids can work through:

1. Identify the main concepts in the DQ by selecting nouns essential to the meaning and answering the question (photosynthesis, plants, AI-powered solution, client, etc.). If they're having trouble settling on a topic, allow them to explore the PBL+ Resources for Special Interests and Passion Projects for ideas (linked via QR Code on page 108).

2. Learn the major concepts in and out and the problems they help solve. Also identify the known or possible causes that may prevent success. For example, AI refers to computer systems with capabilities to perform tasks that typically require human intelligence. AI can improve online shopping, queries, and tracing and prevent fraud—across various sectors many organizations need assistance navigating AI-empowered systems. AI engineers can develop tools, systems, and processes to automate complex tasks for small businesses.

3. Given their new knowledge about the concepts, students can then identify a problem that needs solving or an entity that needs assistance (e.g., local plants, a garden or landscape, or a small local business requiring AI technology).

Step 3: Learn From an Expert

Teachers are the masters of the content they teach—but may not necessarily be fully aware of how professionals apply it authentically (Wolpert-Gawron, 2019). Now that students know the problem they want to solve, they can learn more in this phase by seeking an industry expert(s) to partner with (Valenzuela, 2022a). Sometimes teachers know good candidates, and sometimes learners must help in the search. Students can begin by identifying experts from their local community who work at or own organizations or businesses dedicated to solving similar problems to the one they want to solve. Once they've identified possible prospects, they should run their list by their teacher for appropriate vetting. After deciding, the teacher should make initial contact with experts and invite them to the classroom to provide their expertise to the students. If you have trouble finding someone local or able to visit, virtual correspondence is an excellent option for meetings.

Step 4: Develop a Solution That Matters

With the help of experts, students can now begin to seek solutions to the problem they want to solve. Problem-solving is a journey, and it makes all the difference when students can learn from someone who knows how to accomplish what they're seeking to do. It's important to reinforce in this step that their solutions should matter to them and, therefore, to others who want to achieve something similar. Whether creating a piece of music, developing software, or cultivating healthy plants, leveraging experts' knowledge exposes kids to the systems, tools, and frameworks they use in their work. The important thing that learners should emphasize about the solution(s) they create is that someone else should be inspired and able to replicate it. They should explain the details of their transfer so that others can repeat their process and success.

Examples of making their solutions accessible to others may come in the product or performance task they create—such as how-to videos, step-by-step instructions, and making the solution matter through a call to action (CTA). A

CTA can underpin a speech or piece of writing or come in a slogan that requests or encourages people to take action about a problem or important cause (Valenzuela, 2021d). We explored CTAs in Chapter 8 on page 97. Some examples of solutions that matter that kids can develop and map out for others as part of their special interests' projects may include the following:

- Outlining the coding process during app development
- Creating meal plans and workout routines
- Inviting others to recycle
- Reducing digital footprints
- Using blockchain technology
- Composing a song
- Playing an instrument
- Designing a piece of clothing
- Developing a marketing campaign

Step 5: Explain the Solution Publicly

Thus far, students have been engaged—they've worked hard to explore concepts, learned from experts, and developed meaningful solutions. In Step 5, it's time for them to deliver a message to an authentic audience by explaining their solutions to others via a public product. As Chapter 1 on page 17 explains, "public product" is the culminating event at the end of a project that serves as an opportunity for students to showcase their learning. Remember, the solutions they're presenting must matter to others so choose the audience carefully, such as community members, other youth (e.g., peers, students), industry experts, local politicians, parents, and school and district administrators (Valenzuela, 2021d). This step is a powerful culmination of the engagement process in PBL and performance task development because students become motivated to put their best polish on work they know others will view and, most importantly, benefit from.

It's vital for students to carefully craft an impactful and informative session for those in attendance of the public product. They must be mindful of who's in the audience and the message they want to leave them with. The best way to select an audience is to consider who needs and would appreciate this information the most—then set out to organize a presentation with a compelling intro, middle, and end. The audience will need to see the students' research into the solution(s), their application, and the lessons learned. I will expand on how to prepare students for the public product using presentation scripts in Chapter 11, starting on page 128. The important thing for your students to consider is being intentional about what they want to share about their learning so that the audience understands and receives it well.

Not that they're always necessary, but CTAs work well here—especially if students want to make an impact outside the classroom by making their community aware of how to act around critical social issues. For example, students can encourage participation in environmental events such as coastal cleanup or a food drive to feed the needy. CTAs are simple to create and can read like these:

- "Join our conservation club every Wednesday after school to Protect Our Environment."
- "Come to our class food drive to help the needy this Saturday."

Undoubtedly, CTAs are a powerful takeaway for the audience—they are also helpful in providing student presenters with a culminating message and explanation to end their presentation. Also, they continue the project by involving others in future activities.

FIGURE 9.2   5-STEP ORGANIZER FOR PBL+ SPECIAL INTEREST PROJECT

STEP 1: BEGIN WITH A COMPELLING HOOK (1–2 DAYS)	
1. What is the special interest* you'll be exploring and learning about in this project? *PBL+ Resources for Special Interests and Passion Projects for ideas (https://bit.ly/3EPGOOS)*	
2. Do you have any questions or comments about the driving question (DQ) and do you understand the purpose of this project?	
3. Do you have any questions about the project or any of the resources presented during the compelling hook activity?	
4. Reflect on your first team meeting and your shared agreements. What went well and what didn't? How can you help improve the team? What role are you assuming and what task are you completing for this project?	
5. What critical documents will you need to complete your work successfully? List them in this document if you need to (rubric, task list, presentation script, etc.).	
STEP 2: EXPLORE MAJOR CONCEPT(S)	
Use this space to describe what you're learning about the special interest you've selected to explore. • Why does this topic matter to you? • What are some of the major concepts within this topic? • Which concept interests you the most? • What problem(s) need(s) solutions for the concept you've selected? • What problem are you going to develop a solution for?	

STEP 3: LEARN FROM AN EXPERT

You should know the problem you want to solve and can begin seeking out an industry expert(s) in this phase of the project to learn and partner with. Research good professionals in your area but don't contact them directly—present your search to your teacher (who will make contact for you).

If you're still unsure, here are some questions that can help guide your search:

- What is the job title of the professional who solves similar problems to the one I'm attempting to solve?
- What will I need to know and do to develop a solution to the problem?
- Has anyone else tried to solve this problem, and how were they successful?
- Does this industry expert work locally, and how can they be contacted (by email, phone, etc.)?

STEP 4: DEVELOP A SOLUTION THAT MATTERS

Develop and refine your solution(s) to the problem you're attempting to solve. It's important to document your design process as it will come in handy for explaining your work. Here are some considerations:

- Consider how your solution answers the driving question (DQ).
- Why and for whom is your solution important?
- Can you map out your solution steps in a logical and coherent way so someone else can replicate them and get similar results?

STEP 5: EXPLAIN THE SOLUTION PUBLICLY

The following are important considerations for refining how you present your work publicly. Here are some considerations to ensure you have a compelling message and polish your work:

- Who in your community will benefit most from being invited to view your work?

(Continued)

(Continued)

STEP 5: EXPLAIN THE SOLUTION PUBLICLY	
• Create a presentation script to organize your message (consider the beginning, middle, and end). • Compose a compelling call to action (CTA) if applicable. A CTA can underpin your speech or writing or come in a slogan that requests or encourages your audience to take action about a problem or important cause.	

REFLECTION	
Take a moment to reflect after your project is complete. Remember this powerful John Dewey quote: "We do not learn from experience . . . we learn from reflecting on experience." • What did you learn about your topic or special interest? Are you going to pursue learning more about it? • How did you contribute to your team's synergy? • What were your biggest takeaways? • What would you do differently?	

 Available for download at resources.corwin.com/ProjectBasedLearning+

SUMMARY

Engagement in the classroom doesn't just happen—it must be planned and well thought out. Teachers who understand the factors influencing student engagement (communication, collaboration, positive interactions, and timely feedback; DeVito, 2016) are well equipped to inspire their students to carry out project work. After reading the research component of this chapter, readers should consider the many ways of activating engagement to boost academic achievement and performance.

Furthermore, when trying the three engagement strategies, *open your mail, create positive vibes, and use relevant question prompts*, along with the five-step process for rigorous PBL, keep going even if your initial facilitations don't go smoothly. It'll take time to get everyone (including you) doing new things— honor your learners, yourself, and the process. Now that we have engagement strategies and a process for students to follow, let's learn how students can learn good collaboration and teamwork skills in Chapter 10.

CHAPTER 10

....

FOSTERING COLLABORATION AND TEAMWORK

Students working in teams to solve problems and accomplish tasks is a hallmark of project-based learning (PBL) (Valenzuela, 2022a). Like anything else in the PBL classroom, effective teamwork must be taught, modeled, learned, and reflected on. Adults know that working with others isn't always easy—conflict and disagreements are part of relationships. Still, there must be ways for youth working together to remember their commitments to one another, even as emotions run high. When difficulties arise, effective collaboration is only possible with individuals committing to shared agreements and goals and remaining on common ground. In his book *The 7 Habits of Highly Effective People*, Dr. Stephen R. Covey writes about the habit of synergy: "The essence of synergy is to value differences—to respect them, to build on strengths, to compensate for weaknesses" (p. 341).

Often, I find that teachers new to PBL struggle with helping their learners assemble teams and establishing a culture of good collaboration and communication. As a result, establishing teamwork and teaching students to communicate respectfully and effectively with one another is a topic that frequently gets asked about in PBL+ workshop sessions. My response is to consistently leverage what they already do but flip it toward the positive outcomes we want to see in them. For example, students arranging to steal a test or joining together to bully a peer are already collaborating and communicating with one another—unfortunately, not for positive reasons. We, the adults, must remember that often they're mimicking what they see others do on social media and even some adults in their communities. Teachers can use a few simple, but well-calculated, steps from this chapter to reframe their teamwork skills.

> When teaching students new to PBL, I like to implement each of the steps outlined in the subsequent sections.

THE IDEAL TEAMMATE ACTIVITY

Giving learners a point of reference about what's acceptable and what isn't is critical to helping them understand how to work well with others. So, before the students form teams, it's essential to establish guidelines and criteria for being a good teammate—especially if they haven't participated in group work or had a bad prior experience. For this purpose, I created an activity I call "The Ideal Teammate." The activity is meant to prompt reflection and conversations, get learners on the same page, and plant the seeds of fruitful collaboration. Below are some steps you can take with students:

1. Have them create their own definition of teamwork and explain why each individual can help make or break a team. This can be done in a share-out format and kept somewhat informal.

2. Individually, have them capture their thoughts for both "ideal qualities" and "not ideal qualities" of a teammate. These can be written on two separate sticky notes by each student. In my experience, kids like to identify a team member's ideal and not-so-ideal qualities—so much so that I have often been surprised by what they know and offer suggestions.

3. They can then post their sticky notes on a large T-chart (see Figure 10.1).

FIGURE 10.1 THE IDEAL TEAMMATE ACTIVITY

Ideal Qualities	Not Ideal Qualities
Communicator Punctual Flexible	Never on time Apathy Irresponsible
Reliable Leader Honest	Won't share in workload

IMAGE SOURCE: iStock.com/PeterHermesFurian

4. Engage them in a group discussion to establish the qualities of an "Ideal Teammate." Ensure that every voice is heard in the class and that each student understands the vital role they will play in effective and successful teamwork. In this step, the class must reach a consensus about what constitutes ideal teammates. These qualities can be discussed again as needed. Discussion prompts may include the following:

   - What are your main takeaways from the ideal teammate activity?

   - Why is effective collaboration critical for product development?

   - What are the indicators of effective collaboration? Think of the ideal qualities.

   - Which ideal teammate qualities do you already possess and which one(s) could you improve?

   - How can we leverage the inventory we created of the ideal and not-so-ideal teammate qualities when one of our team members needs a nudge?

I like to keep the T-chart displayed in the classroom and point to it regularly when any student needs a reminder. I have also seen learners point to it to remind one another about the dos and don'ts of good teamwork.

SET ROLES FOR EACH TEAM MEMBER

Setting roles for each team member provides every learner with purpose and ownership over specific project tasks. It also provides and sets a timeline for completing their assigned task(s) (see Figure 10.2 for the PBL+ Team Task List that follows this section) and lets them know what they will be graded on upon project completion. That doesn't mean that each student will know how to complete their required task(s) without assistance, but it explicitly informs them of their responsibilities and project deliverables. I have personally seen how empowering it is for students when they're assigned roles in project work. Here are the top three reasons with explanations.

1. It gives students ownership of a job and contribution to the team's overall work and the final product(s). This is important for students who thrive with and crave structure. They always want to know their duties and value the clarity of their workflow and intended commitments. For students who feel isolated and unseen, setting a role for them is empowering because it helps them feel like they belong and contribute positively and in meaningful ways. This experience may be the jumpstart they need for a future job or career.

2. Students glean how different careers use different workers to come together to complete tasks, problem-solve, design, and conjure up solutions. For example, many projects I implemented with students were computer science themed. For authenticity, learners assumed roles typical of the software development industry, such as software engineers (project managers), software developers, and programmers. By implementing multiple projects throughout the school year, everyone had the opportunity to try their hand at each role.

Teachers should help students understand the various roles within professional teams in the different professions and industries they're assuming in the project(s) (engineering, health and medical, music production, etc.). Consulting with a professional during the planning phase of your PBL unit can give you the needed insight for pinpointing accurate roles in professions.

3. Students receive a grade for the actual work they've completed instead of getting the same grade as all of their team members. This prevents many kids from participating in future projects or schoolwork involving group work. For example, my daughter went to a PBL school and continually expressed frustration with doing most of her team's work, but everyone still received the same grade. Her sentiments told me that teamwork needed a little more clarity—not necessarily that the project was poorly designed.

Use a task list to keep track of task completion and who's doing what. Without a task list, it's challenging for kids to keep track of their work and for teachers to grade a team of students justly. Team members must realize that there are two due dates—one for the final product and the other for the task they've been assigned. I created the following task list to help you organize your teams on the completion of their tasks.

FIGURE 10.2 PBL+ TEAM TASK LIST TEMPLATE

Project Name:			
Product:		**Due Date:**	
Teammates:			
TASK	DUE DATE	ASSIGNEE	STATUS

online resources ⟋ Available for download at resources.corwin.com/ProjectBasedLearning+

FIRST TEAM MEETING: CREATE SHARED AGREEMENTS

A first team meeting is essential for getting everyone on the same page about how they will work together. If your class is new to PBL, I highly encourage you to complete this step. When framed correctly, PBL teachers can mold learners into highly functional, synergistic, and happy teams working on completing their best possible products. Doing so isn't easy when students haven't had good prior experiences to draw from, but it's possible. Creating synergy is complex and requires communal relationships (Psychology, n.d.) anchored by norms and expectations valued and upheld by each team member. Having student teams spend time developing a set of shared norms and agreements shouldn't be neglected.

Consider how relationships work in the adult world: Sometimes we have to sit with partners, spouses, or colleagues to agree on how we collaborate. Youth should also leverage the power of this practice. Every learner should feel that their input matters to their teammates. This can begin with all hearts, minds, and hands outlining how they will work together. Student teams should therefore take time to collaboratively create a set of shared agreements before focusing on other priorities of project work. To be engaged synergistically, people need to know what others require from them and vice versa (Rigoni & Nelson, 2016). PBL offers an opportunity to get kids started before beginning their professional lives.

SETTING GUIDELINES FOR STUDENTS WORKING TOGETHER

Shared agreements, also called working agreements, community agreements, or shared expectations, are guidelines and norms that define how a group ideally wants to work together and what they wish to experience in their working environment (Haskell, 2013). Creating the agreements can also allow willing learners to communicate and empathize with their teammates appropriately and effectively. In PBL classrooms, student teams that take the time to create their shared agreements collectively see more success in the following:

- Establishing and maintaining better norms for learning in community
- Effectively using the time and talents of their team members
- Respecting and valuing each other's thoughts and ideas
- Articulating clear project goals and individual task responsibilities
- Providing healthy parameters for difficult discussions and problem-solving

Before commencing with this strategy, teachers should inform learners that having a set of norms and shared agreements does not mean teams can solve every problem immediately, especially when tackling complex ones. It's also important to consider that just because the team skillfully solves a challenge, it doesn't mean other problems won't soon need the group's attention. The good news is that they experienced success activating their shared norms and guidelines for tough problem-solving.

Engaging in group work requires a lot of trust, and establishing trust isn't easy for everyone—especially for those who've felt let down in the past. You may find that some fence-mending will need to happen first. In that case, encourage youth to settle differences and offer mediation if needed. Disagreements during a project can lead to heightened emotions and a student may break one or more of their team's agreements. It's OK. Kids are human—they are not a set of norms. When this happens, it's fine to table discussion and reconvene when agreements can be upheld.

5 WAYS TO BEGIN CREATING SHARED AGREEMENTS

1. **Cover the basics.** Teachers can get kids started by uplifting a few basic agreements that correspond to all. Examples may include some of the following:
   - Everyone participates.
   - Critique work, not each other.
   - Try to settle differences internally, and, as a last resort, take it to the teacher.
   - Lead with empathy and self-awareness.
   - Listen to understand, not to respond.

2. **Address must-haves and deal-breakers.** Individually each team member can begin reflecting on their must-haves and deal-breakers in an ideal work environment. Teachers can have everyone capture their thoughts on a piece of paper folded down the middle for about 5 to 7 minutes. Upon completion of a first draft, I advise them to revise their list realistically, only leaving non-negotiable items. This is powerful for visualizing thinking and opening honest discussions.

3. **Discuss the culture you're building.** Allow team members to speak from the heart to explain the observable behaviors and culture they would like to see happen due to creating the shared agreements. Don't rush this if possible—allow them the air space to engage in dialogue.

4. **Get everyone involved.** On large chart paper using markers, welcome each team to add one or two agreements. After all the agreements are captured, have each team consolidate for redundancy and make a manageable list.

5. **Share your agreements.** Once the list is refined, it can become a contract that everyone signs (see Figure 10.3 for the handout). The agreements

FIGURE 10.3 PBL+ SHARED AGREEMENTS CONTRACT TEMPLATE

Project Name:	
Teammate Signatures:	
Date:	
Our Shared Agreements	
1. Everyone participates.	
2. Critique work, not each other.	
3. Try to settle differences internally, and as a last resort, take it to the teacher.	
4. Lead with empathy and self-awareness.	
5. Listen to understand, not to respond.	

 Available for download at resources.corwin.com/ProjectBasedLearning+

should then be posted virtually or be easily accessible in spaces where the team(s) meets regularly (e.g., group binder). I like to have teams silently scan and reflect on their list at the start of their work meetings. This brief practice allows anyone to discuss how the agreements are being upheld before proceeding with their daily task(s).

Creating shared agreements will take some time on the front end—especially in spaces where open discussion isn't practiced regularly. Once young people establish trust with one another, activating their shared norms becomes significant in producing a productive and interdependent work environment.

TEAM-BUILDING ACTIVITIES AND COLLABORATION MEASURES

Team-building activities are optional but are an excellent way to prepare learners new to PBL to work with their teammates. For teachers, team-building activities can serve two purposes:

1. Help learners practice problem-solving strategies together

2. Have learners assess their collaboration skills using a single-point rubric

For this purpose, you can use any team-building activities you already use in your class. PBS Kids (n.d.) has many fantastic, easy-to-implement STEM activities if you need some inspiration. Although tempting, you should refrain from introducing the collaboration skills rubric (see Figure 10.4) to students as they work because you want them to create a point of reference for when the rubric is introduced.

After the team-building activity, provide them with the rubric and instruct each student team to read through the indicators together and provide the following:

•   Two or three things they did at "proficient" or "highly proficient"

•   Three things they did at "emerging" along with a correction plan for future group work

Let each team take turns expressing their experience working together in the activity and encourage them to use language from the collaboration skills rubric. You can close the activity by engaging them in low-stakes and fruitful dialogue by allowing each group to share out and provide how they would improve their collaboration skills throughout the remainder of the project.

FIGURE 10.4 PBL+ SINGLE-POINT COLLABORATION SKILLS RUBRIC

EMERGING	PROFICIENT	HIGHLY PROFICIENT	
1–3	4	5	
Provide feedback for improvement	Expectations met Provide feedback for improvement	Provide feedback for improvement	SCORE
	I can take responsibility for myself by being prepared to work, complete tasks in a timely manner without reminders, and use feedback from my teammates.		/5
	I can help my team solve problems, manage conflict, and make dialogue and brainstorming effective by providing well-thought-out feedback and ideas.		/5
	I can respect my teammates by being polite, kind, helpful, and respectful of their views and ideas, and when I don't agree do so diplomatically.		/5
	I can complete the duties assigned to me on the task list, set schedules, adhere to deadlines, and use time effectively.		/5
Total			/20

 Available for download at resources.corwin.com/ProjectBasedLearning+

SUMMARY

Sometimes our students will come to us needing as much help with their collaboration skills as they do with the content we teach. As discussed in Chapter 9, effective collaboration, like engagement, doesn't just happen. It must be planned for and well orchestrated, especially in spaces where working together isn't the norm. Taking time to help students learn essential life skills through the intentional strategies in this chapter can lay the groundwork for our classroom/culture, helps learners capture the content, and helps them develop into better citizens. We will now close out this section of our book with tips for helping them prepare for their presentations in the final product.

CHAPTER 11

....

HELPING STUDENTS PREPARE FOR THE PUBLIC PRODUCT

In Chapter 1 we briefly learned that in project-based learning (PBL), the public product holds great significance and is the culminating project. I also recommend teachers cap off performance tasks with a public presentation to an authentic audience. Remember, an authentic audience may include community members, other youth, industry experts, local politicians, parents, and school and district administrators (Valenzuela, 2021d). The public product is, therefore, a genuine opportunity for you and your students to show others outside the four walls of your classroom their great work and accomplishments. Although the public product does not have to be students making a formal presentation, presenting and speaking about their work to others is a vital skill to have long after they leave K–12 schooling.

However, not every student is comfortable speaking publicly—learning to do so is a skill that is honed over time. When kids do not have experience explaining what they have learned to others, they typically become anxious and nervous about doing so. When this happens to my students, I always encourage them to practice and tell them that "practice may not always make us perfect—but it sure makes us better." So, if your students feel apprehensive or stuck on how to present or even what to say next, the trick is to create ample opportunities for them to start practicing during your PBL units. Here are four steps you can take to help them improve over time gradually while building their capacity for performing in low- to high-stakes settings.

STEP 1: USE PROTOCOLS THAT REQUIRE STUDENTS TO EXPLAIN

Preparing students to speak in front of others begins with having them practice speaking in class frequently, but it's not that simple—teachers need strategies to do it right. Singling out students to speak in front of others, even to classmates, can backfire if they don't feel comfortable, and may harm their confidence in sharing their work. Apprehensive students can benefit from using educational protocols as speaking structures when learning to present their work. An educational protocol is a well-defined set of structured step-by-step actions teachers and students use for a specific academic purpose (EL Education, n.d.-a). When I use protocols, something magical happens: My classroom culture becomes more collaborative and kids become better engaged and more confident in transferring their knowledge to others.

I recommend using speaking protocols regularly, even when we're not teaching projects. With repetition, everyone can learn to focus on learning to dialogue effectively in small low-stakes groups. I find that this practice prepares them for much bigger audiences that they will encounter later. Say Something and Jigsaws are two protocols you can use for helping your learners explain their learning. The Say Something protocol (EL Education, 2013) is great for getting students used to explaining their thoughts about a shared reading (see Figure 11.1).

FIGURE 11.1 THE STEPS TO THE SAY SOMETHING PROTOCOL

PROCESS	TIME	PERSON(S)
Procedure In pairs or triads, students will select a common text and choose stopping a point(s) to take turns to "say something."	2 Minutes	Teacher and Students
Explain Tell students what they will say to each other when they reach the stopping point. For example, a question, a summary, a critical issue, an interesting idea, or a new connection.	2 Minutes	Teacher
Model Provide two examples of what a student can say to peers at each stopping point. Ensure all modeled statements or questions are concise, well thought out, and related to the text.	2 Minutes	Teacher
Read Have student groups read a common text.	3 Minutes	Students
Stop and Say Something Once student partners have reached the selected stopping point, they each take turns to "say something" to each other about what they read. *This step should be repeated until the end of the entire reading.*	5 Minutes	Students
Whole-Group Debrief After the reading is complete, engage the whole group in discussing the text.	5 Minute	Teacher and Students
Total	19 Minutes	

SOURCE: Adapted from EL Education by Jorge Valenzuela of Lifelong Learning Defined, Inc.

 Available for download at resources.corwin.com/ProjectBasedLearning+

In Step 2, I model using sentence stems that help my learners respond better to the readings, for example (Heick, n.d.):

- The character mentioned that . . .
- Overall, what the author is trying to say is . . .
- I agree with the position she/he took because . . .
- I'm confused about when the author wrote. . . . Can you help clarify?

The Jigsaw protocol is great for chunking and unpacking informational text in student-led expert teams (see Figure 11.2). Jigsaw activities can be leveraged to create informal opportunities that allow students to explain targeted topics to classmates. Have one group of students become "experts" in an aspect of a topic, then share what they know in jigsawed groups with others who learned about different parts of the topic. I structure this by asking them to offer their own definitions and provide evidence from the reading(s), while explaining it all casually.

FIGURE 11.2   THE STEPS TO THE JIGSAW PROTOCOL

PROCESS	TIME	PERSON(S)
Jigsaw Text and Form Expert Teams Chunk a selected text into manageable and smaller parts and form homogeneous expert student groups. Assign a portion of the selected text to each expert team.	2 Minute	Teacher and Students
Read, Analyze, and Explain Student expert teams read and analyze text (annotating, highlighting, etc.) and explain their learning with each other.	10 Minutes	Students
Synthesize Expert teams create a synthesis in the form of an artifact with three bullets: (1) concept(s) defined, (2) examples from the reading, and (3) explanation of their main takeaways. Students who struggle with writing can create graphics or images.	6 Minutes	Students
Teach Others Have all expert teams return to the heterogeneous group (e.g., the entire class) to present and discuss their learning.	2 Minutes	Teacher and Students
Complete the Jigsaw Students reconvene in their homogeneous expert groups to align the learning from the other jigsaw pieces of text they learned from the other expert teams.	5 Minutes	Students
Total	25 Minutes	

SOURCE: Adapted from the Jigsaw Classroom by Jorge Valenzuela of Lifelong Learning Defined, Inc.

 Available for download at resources.corwin.com/ProjectBasedLearning+

As you implement the protocols with students, they may be tempted to skip steps or speak over each other. To ensure they honor the protocols, model their use frequently and circle the classroom during implementation for students to feel your presence. Always stress to your students the importance of structure and practice.

STEP 2: HELP STUDENTS DEVELOP PRESENTATION SCRIPTS

Consistently using the tools and dedication to the principles in Step 1 in the previous section will ensure that many learners become much more comfortable using academic language and discussing their learning with others. However, many will still need more scaffolding to organize better what they want to say for the public product. Scaffolding refers to methods and tools teachers use to support students as they learn new concepts and develop new skills (Grand Canyon University, 2022). Scaffolds often are temporarily put in place and gradually removed as students increase their capacity for the skills they support.

I recommend a presentation script to help organize and prepare their dialogue for the public product (see Figure 11.3). Even your most experienced students will appreciate the presentation script tool as it's an excellent scaffold for organizing their presentations and keeping their audience in mind. They can complete the tool using information gleaned from their companion PBL+ Special Interest Project Planner (see Chapter 9 on page 112), which they've been updating throughout the project. Furthermore, the script assists them with mapping out what they will say at the beginning, middle, and end of their presentations, along with what they will show or do to capture the audience's attention. Once their scripts are to their liking, be sure to dedicate time to allow them to rehearse, explaining what they wrote both in class and at home.

FIGURE 11.3 PBL+ PRESENTATION SCRIPT TEMPLATE

Beginning of Presentation: (Team introduces themselves and the project purpose by stating the driving question)

"Hello, my name is _____ and my name is _____ and my name is _____."

"We are _____ graders in Mr./Ms. (teacher's name) class at (school name)."

"The project we participated in is '(project title)' and we answered the driving question: (insert driving question)."

Driving Question example: "How can we as computational thinkers design a children's game that teaches younger peers foundational coding skills and the use of electronic circuits?"

Middle of Presentation: (Team explains their project role, the career field they learned about, and the product they created, along with its purpose and how the audience can also participate)

"In my role of (insert role of student) I learned from an expert about the (insert career field, e.g., engineering, health and medical) field and _____
_____."

"Our team created a (insert the final product) to (the problem the product solves) _____

_____."

Sentence Starters:

- "This (insert product) can also be utilized in various ways, which include _____

_____."

- "We also created a (insert additional artifacts, e.g., a graph) to demonstrate _____

_____."

- "Our (insert product) helps our community by _____ and you can also

  participate by _____."

- The code in our game design makes the _____ do _____

_____.

End of Presentation: (Team explains their major takeaways, fields questions from the audience, and thanks them for participating)

"Our main takeaway(s) from our work included _____

_____."

Q/A Sentence Starters:

- "We will now open the floor for audience questions."

- "If anyone has any questions we are happy to answer them now."

Closing:

- "Thank you for attending our presentation today."

STEP 3: TAKE PRESSURE OFF STUDENTS WHILE PRESENTING

My teaching experience has taught me that learners gain absolute confidence after consistently failing forward and eventually experiencing successive successful moments. For students who don't have much previous experience presenting publicly, you will need to find a way to help them combat their anxiety levels come presentation day. I recommend gauging how they feel about showcasing first. For those with high anxiety levels, limit pressure as much as possible—not doing so will make them dislike projects. Reassure them that it's perfectly normal to feel nervous speaking in public and remind them that practice will improve their skills. Additionally, let them know that presenting ideas, information, and their work to others is an important career and success skill to develop.

Drawing inspiration from the Carousel activity protocol (NCTE, n.d.), I created a simple format you can use to remove tension from students. To implement the protocol well, create presentation stations where students present their work in a large circle resembling a carousel. Make sure to leave ample space between each station because it can get loud. When it's showtime, organize all of your

Here's a link to a video of my students presenting in the Carousel format: bit.ly/3YvWqyN

visitors (the public) into equal groups and have them move from station to station every four to six minutes. Each team can be permitted four minutes to present their work and two minutes for Q&A (see Figure 11.4). To ease anxieties further, I recommend that the first adults that students share their product with are their parents or caregivers, family members, or guests they invited. I have found that by doing this, their confidence increases round by round.

FIGURE 11.4   THE CAROUSEL ACTIVITY PROTOCOL

Setup	Teams set up and prepare to present to audience members.	1 Minute
Presentation	Students present and audience members take notes.	4 Minutes
Q/A	Audience members ask questions and students respond.	2 Minutes
Rotate	Audience goes to next presenting group.	1 Minute
Repeat	Repeat the steps above until audience members see all student presentations.	__ Minutes

 Available for download at resources.corwin.com/ProjectBasedLearning+

STEP 4: LEAD BY GOING FIRST

As teachers, we are the leaders in our classrooms, and being the leader means going first. Teachers must be the first presenter/moderator of discussions both before and after the students present their public products. This shows them that we are in it together and has enabled me to gain my students' and stakeholders' confidence, trust, commitment, and respect. The teacher's opening presentation doesn't have to be very long or require much airtime—five minutes is enough. All we have to do is welcome parents and stakeholders, provide some context for why we're doing our work, and explain the format of how the presentations will be conducted.

Here's a video modeling how to set up student presentations by opening the event and being the first speaker: bit.ly/3T3xMVe

Here's a video of me modeling the closing discussion and reflections: bit.ly/3lZc5B4

After the kids present, I also recommend leading a final discussion/reflection with both the kids and adults who participated. This part doesn't have to be very long, either. Still, it allows you to revisit the learned topics, make critical connections, guide the celebration of learning, and promote the fantastic student work in your classroom.

SUMMARY

Getting learners ready to speak in public confidently is often overlooked in projects and performance tasks—mainly due to the time it takes to prepare them adequately to perform at their best. It requires trust, collaboration, easy-to-follow steps, protocols, and lots of practice. Let the advice, protocols, sentence stems, and presentation script in this chapter scaffold the process for you and your students. Use affirmations often and model what you want to see in them. When they fail, remind them it's part of the learning and success process. Always lead by example and utilize the elements in the PBL+ Framework to guide and strengthen your PBL journey.

EPILOGUE

Thank you, reader, for taking the time to read and implement this book's many research-informed recommendations. Undoubtedly, Project-Based Learning+ (PBL+) encompasses the many skills, processes, tools, and protocols that promote learning and create academic, social, and emotional success for all kids—especially those who are historically underserved (children of color and from low-income families).

PBL is not just about completing projects; it's also about setting goals, honoring commitments, persevering through the complexities of learning, and synergizing with others. It's an instructional approach I hope serves you and your students as much as it has done for my learners and me.

Countless data collections over the years informed the elements of the PBL+ Framework. Teachers can use the Framework to support both academic and social and emotional learning (SEL) for students with diverse needs and backgrounds by implementing its steps consistently and with fidelity.

Adapting the Framework can also improve your teaching practice by strengthening your core instruction and implementing high-yielding teaching strategies. I hope the projects I present in Part 2 of this book begin as inspiration and that my suggested design methodology becomes the impetus for teachers to plan more intentionally.

I urge school leaders to take the advice in this book and acquire my sustainable PBL+ professional learning through Corwin for the teachers in their schools. Doing so will ensure that projects and performance tasks are designed and implemented successfully.

Being effective requires collaboration, time, patience, and love. It's an investment in our teachers, students, country (wherever that may be), and humanity.

With gratitude,

Jorge

APPENDIX A

Project and Performance Task Planner Template

Title:

Content Area:

Grade Level:

Duration:

1. **Standards to be Assessed** (2–5 standards): *Identify specific Standards of Learning (<u>CCSS</u> or <u>SOLs</u>).* **Literacy Connection(s)** **Numeracy Connection(s)**	2. **Learning Intentions:** *Student-friendly statements identifying the observable or measurable outcomes desired.*
3. **Performance Task Situation or Project Description:** *Describe the task(s) to be assessed. What major concept(s) will students explore and conjure a solution(s) to complete the task?*	
4. **Product(s) and/or Performance Task:** *What will students produce as evidence of attainment of learning intentions?*	

(Continued)

(Continued)

5. **Authentic Audience:**

The audience comprises individuals interested in the findings and products that students create. There may be a call to action for the audience to assist with the project made by the presenter(s).

6. **Student Role(s):**

The role provides the student with the opportunity to assume the career role or job associated with accomplishing the goal(s) of the project or performance task.

7. **Driving Question (DQ):**

This unit plan's central question, used to guide students throughout the learning process.

8. **Alignment Tool for Student Task Instructions and Teaching:**

Use the following alignment tool to organize formative assessments and lessons/scaffolds for each learning intention. Also, consider which learning activities align best with the intended standards and outcomes, the completion timeline, and the materials or resources students need. See Table 4.1 in Chapter 4 for a completed example.

PRODUCT(S) AND TASKS	LEARNING INTENTIONS AND PACING	FORMAL AND INFORMAL FORMATIVE ASSESSMENTS	MINI-LESSONS, HIGH-YIELDING STRATEGIES, AND SCAFFOLDS

9. Scoring:

Single-point rubric tool for scoring products and performance tasks. See Table 5.1 in Chapter 5 for a completed example.

EMERGING 1–3 PROVIDE FEEDBACK FOR IMPROVEMENT	PROFICIENT 4 GRADE-LEVEL EXPECTATIONS MET PROVIDE FEEDBACK FOR IMPROVEMENT	HIGHLY PROFICIENT 5 PROVIDE FEEDBACK FOR IMPROVEMENT	SCORE
	I have . . . (Standard #)		/5
	I have . . . (Standard #)		/5
	I have . . . (Standard #)		/5
	I have . . . (Standard #)		/5
Total			/20

10. Student Engagement and Academic Achievement Monitoring:

Monitor engagement by asking questions and leading discussions, observing participation in collaborative work by seeing how students respond in smaller settings, and polling students using engagement surveys.

Academic achievement should be monitored daily using formative assessments. Good ones for strengthening core instruction may include thumbs-up responses, exit tickets, and quizzes. Biweekly, end-of-unit, and benchmark assessments are metrics your district may have in place for you to use.

11. Teacher Reflection for Understanding Your Own Impact:

Following implementation, consider how learning experiences can be improved in future iterations of this project.

Surveying, polling, and student conferences can help improve teaching impact. You might ask questions such as the following:

- *Which classroom activities help you learn most?*

- *What changes do you recommend I make to help you learn better?*

- *What motivates you to learn most?*

- *What can I do better?*

SOURCE: Inspired by GRASP Model by Jay McTighe. By Lifelong Learning Defined, Inc.

 Available for download at resources.corwin.com/ProjectBasedLearning+

APPENDIX B

The Responsible Decision-Making Project and Performance Task Template

Title: The Responsible Decision-Making Project: Spreading Awareness Through Campaigns

Content Area: ELA (Adaptable by Multiple Areas)

Grade Level: 6–12

Duration: 3.5–4 Weeks

1. **Standards to be Assessed** (2–5 standards):	2. **Learning Intentions:**
Identify specific Standards of Learning (CCSS or SOLs) and SEL competencies.	*Student-friendly statements identifying the observable or measurable outcomes desired.*
• **CCSS.ELA-LITERACY.W.9-10.1.B:** Develop claim(s) and counterclaims fairly, supplying evidence for each while pointing out the strengths and limitations of both in a manner that anticipates the audience's knowledge level and concerns. • **CCSS.ELA-LITERACY.SL.9-10.4:** Present information, findings, and supporting evidence clearly, concisely, and logically such that listeners can follow the line of reasoning and the organization, development, substance, and style are appropriate to purpose, audience, and task. • **CCSS.ELA-LITERACY.RI.9-10.7:** Analyze various accounts of a subject told in different mediums (e.g., a person's life story in both print and multimedia), determining which details are emphasized in each account.	• I can complete a decision-making matrix to help me analyze multiple choices with possible outcomes. • I can identify two to three possible decisions for a given situation. • I can weigh each decision's pros and cons to determine the most responsible choice. • I can add and subtract positive and negative numbers using a number line. • I can make thoughtful and informed decisions based on the information I have gathered and analyzed. • I can communicate my decision and explain my rationale for making it to others. • I can survey my classmates and school community members to decide on a significant issue that will be addressed in my campaign.

(Continued)

(Continued)

- **CCSS.ELA-LITERACY.W.9-10.6:** Use technology, including the internet, to produce, publish, and update individual or shared writing products, taking advantage of technology's capacity to link to other information and to display information flexibly and dynamically.

- **CCSS.MATH.CONTENT.HSA.SSE.A.1.a:** Interpret parts of an expression, such as terms, factors, and coefficients.

- **CCSS.MATH.CONTENT.6.SP.A.1:** Recognize a statistical question as one that anticipates variability in the data related to the question and accounts for it in the answers.

- **CCSS.MATH.CONTENT.7.SP.A.2:** Use data from a random sample to draw inferences about a population with an unknown characteristic of interest. Generate multiple samples (or simulated samples) of the same size to gauge the variation in estimates or predictions.

SEL Connection(s): Responsible decision making includes identifying and analyzing choices and options, considering multiple perspectives, goal setting and planning, recognizing solutions that benefit all parties, and reflection and evaluation.

Literacy Connection(s): Reading and writing, analyzing and evaluating text, summarizing and synthesizing information. Developing claims and counterclaims. Clear communication, analyzing multiple perspectives, and technological literacy.

Numeracy Connection(s): Interpretation of mathematical expressions, identifying statistical questions and inference, and sampling.

- I can understand the issue I am raising awareness about for my campaign.

- I can develop a clear message and call to action for my campaign.

- I can connect the ideas in my campaign to the goal of improving responsible decision-making in my school community.

- I can collaborate with others to create and present engaging content for my campaign.

- I can identify a target audience for my campaign.

- I can use my campaign to teach others the importance of responsible decision making to improve the school climate and culture.

3. **Performance Task Situation or Project Description:**

Learning to make responsible decisions is important for teenagers' personal development and lifelong learning. In this project, students will develop awareness about the science of decision making and learn to use tools that help them evaluate their options using well-thought-out processes involving various age-appropriate scenarios. They will hone their decision-making skills through role-play, class discussions, and creating an impactful campaign with a call to action to raise awareness about issues affecting students at their school. To fully develop their campaigns, they will work in teams to choose and understand a topic, develop a call to action, identify a target audience, and create engaging content to effectively deliver their message publicly.

4. **Product(s) and/or Performance Task:**

- **Responsible Decision-Making Matrix:** Students will complete a decision-making matrix to help them make better decisions between up to three choices by weighing options and evaluating the impact (pros and cons) on themselves and others using a simple point system, with positive numbers for pros and negative ones for cons. After tallying their numbers, the decision with the highest score can be deemed the most responsible one.

- **Awareness Campaign:** Students will collaborate with peers and adults to create an awareness campaign about an issue affecting school community members. They will do the following:

  o Learn the issue inside and out they're raising awareness about.

  o Develop a clear message and call to action.

  o Identify a target audience.

  o Create engaging content such as public service announcements, role-plays, ads, articles, and podcasts.

  o Connect the ideas in their campaigns to improve the school climate by teaching others about the importance of responsible decision making.

5. **Authentic Audience:**

Students target their awareness campaign to an audience of their choice, which may include community members (including family members), other youth (e.g., peers, students), industry experts, local politicians, parents, and school and district administrators. The presentation may also include a call to action for the audience to support the project.

6. **Student Role(s):**

Assuming the role of change advocates and artists, students will use their mural design to:

- Provide empathy to classmates and teachers by understanding how they feel.

- Offer support and resources to others in their class and wider school community.

- Share their knowledge and expertise in a public forum.

7. **Driving Question (DQ):**

Since students are improving their own decision-making skills and in community with others, there will be two DQs for the project. For one DQ, they will answer independently; for the other, they will respond with their classmates.

- *How do I improve my responsible decision-making skills to create better outcomes for both myself and others?*

- *How can we as_____ create a campaign to raise awareness about _____ in order to improve _____ for _____ in our school community? (e.g., "How can we as advocates create a campaign to raise awareness about campus bullying in order to improve safety for all in our school community?")*

8a. **Alignment Tool for Student Task Instructions** and **Teaching:**

Use the following alignment tool to organize formative assessments and lessons/scaffolds for each learning intention. Also, consider which learning activities align best with the intended standards and outcomes, the completion timeline, and the materials or resources students need. See Table 4.1 in Chapter 4 for a completed example.

(Continued)

(Continued)

STUDENT-DEVELOPED PRODUCT	LEARNING INTENTIONS AND PACING	FORMAL AND INFORMAL FORMATIVE ASSESSMENTS	LESSONS, HIGH-YIELDING STRATEGIES, AND SCAFFOLDS
Responsible Decision-Making Matrix **(2 class periods)**	I can complete a decision-making matrix to help me analyze multiple choices with possible outcomes. (2 class periods)	• Brainstorm ideas • Begin developing the responsible decision-making matrix • Responses during classroom discussions • Exit ticket	• Teacher-led mini-lesson explaining major concepts • Teacher modeling use of the decision-making matrix • Responsible decision-making template • All-class discussion and debrief
	• I can identify two to three possible decisions for a given situation. • I can weigh each decision's pros and cons to determine the most responsible choice. • I can add and subtract positive and negative numbers using a number line. (1 class period)	• Teacher-led discussion • Update responsible decision-making matrix • Reflect and revise • Exit ticket	• Teacher modeling decision-making and relevant math skills • Individual and small-group teaching • Responsible decision-making template • Teacher/student feedback • Whole-class reflection
	• I can make thoughtful and informed decisions based on the information I have gathered and analyzed. • I can communicate my decision and explain my rationale for making it to others. (1 class period)	• Update responsible decision-making matrix • Feedback protocol using rubric • Discussion with teacher • Exit ticket	• Individual and small-group teaching • Additional resources pertaining to using the responsible decision-making matrix • Responsible decision-making template • Teacher/student feedback • Whole-class reflection

9a. **Scoring:**

Single-point rubric tool for scoring products and performance tasks. See Table 5.1 in Chapter 5 for a completed example.

EMERGING 1–3 PROVIDE FEEDBACK FOR IMPROVEMENT	PROFICIENT 4 GRADE-LEVEL EXPECTATIONS MET PROVIDE FEEDBACK FOR IMPROVEMENT	HIGHLY PROFICIENT 5 PROVIDE FEEDBACK FOR IMPROVEMENT	SCORE
	I can complete a decision-making matrix to help me analyze multiple choices with possible outcomes. (W.9-10.1.B, SL. 9-10.4, RI.9-10.7)		/5
	I can identify two to three possible decisions for a given situation. (W.9-10.1.B, SL.9-10.4)		/5
	I can weigh each decision's pros and cons to determine the most responsible choice. (Responsible Decision-Making Competency)		/5
	I can add and subtract positive and negative numbers using a number line. (6.SP.A.1)		/5
	I can make thoughtful and informed decisions based on the information I have gathered and analyzed. (Literacy and Numeracy Connections)		/5
	I can communicate my decision and explain my rationale for making it to others. (Literacy Connections)		/5
Total			/30

(Continued)

(Continued)

8b. Alignment Tool for Student Task Instructions and Teaching

STUDENT-DEVELOPED PRODUCT	LEARNING INTENTIONS AND PACING	FORMAL AND INFORMAL FORMATIVE ASSESSMENTS	MINI-LESSONS, HIGH-YIELDING STRATEGIES, AND SCAFFOLDS
Awareness Campaign **(6–8 Class Periods)**	• I can survey my classmates and school community members to decide on a significant issue that will be addressed in my campaign. • I can understand the issue I am raising awareness about for my campaign. (2–3 class periods)	• Explore issues that need solving in the school community • Create survey in Google Forms • Responses during classroom discussions • Exit ticket	• Teacher-led mini-lesson on campaigns and surveying • Teacher modeling • Teacher-curated resources on issues for students to explore • All-class discussion and debrief
	• I can develop a clear message and call to action for my campaign. • I can connect the ideas in my campaign to the goal of improving responsible decision making in my school community. (2 class periods)	• Call to action development • Using and reviewing the responsible decision-making matrix • Responses during classroom discussions • Exit ticket	• Teacher-led mini-lesson on developing calls to action • Responsible decision-making matrix template • Teacher/student feedback • Whole-class reflection
	• I can collaborate with others to create and present engaging content for my campaign. • I can identify a target audience for my campaign. (3–4 class periods)	• Using media and edtech tools • Brainstorming appropriate audience • Reflect and revise • Exit ticket	• Individual and small-group teaching on various edtech and media tools (may be led by experts) • Critique with an expert • Teacher directions and guiding questions • Teacher/student feedback

STUDENT-DEVELOPED PRODUCT	LEARNING INTENTIONS AND PACING	FORMAL AND INFORMAL FORMATIVE ASSESSMENTS	MINI-LESSONS, HIGH-YIELDING STRATEGIES, AND SCAFFOLDS
	• I can use my campaign to teach others the importance of responsible decision making to improve the school climate and culture. (After the project)	• Making the work available to the public (intended audience) • Reflect and revise • Add finishing touches • Exit ticket	• Teacher-led mini-lesson on implementing campaigns • Individual and small-group teaching • Critique with an expert • Teacher/student feedback

9b. **Scoring:**

Single-point rubric tool for scoring products and performance tasks. See Table 5.1 in Chapter 5 for a completed example.

EMERGING 1–3 PROVIDE FEEDBACK FOR IMPROVEMENT	PROFICIENT 4 GRADE-LEVEL EXPECTATIONS MET PROVIDE FEEDBACK FOR IMPROVEMENT	HIGHLY PROFICIENT 5 PROVIDE FEEDBACK FOR IMPROVEMENT	SCORE
	I can survey my classmates and school community members to decide on a significant issue that will be addressed in my campaign. (Social-Awareness and Decision-Making Competencies)		/7
	I can understand the issue I am raising awareness about for my campaign. (SEL and Literacy Connections)		/7

(Continued)

(Continued)

EMERGING 1–3 PROVIDE FEEDBACK FOR IMPROVEMENT	PROFICIENT 4 GRADE-LEVEL EXPECTATIONS MET PROVIDE FEEDBACK FOR IMPROVEMENT	HIGHLY PROFICIENT 5 PROVIDE FEEDBACK FOR IMPROVEMENT	SCORE
	I can develop a clear message and call to action for my campaign. (Literacy Connections)		/7
	I can connect the ideas in my campaign to the goal of improving responsible decision making in my school community. (Literacy and SEL Connections)		/7
	I can collaborate with others to create and present engaging content for my campaign. (Literacy and SEL Connections)		/7
	I can identify a target audience for my campaign. (Social-awareness and SEL Connections)		/7
	I can use my campaign to teach others the importance of responsible decision making to improve the school climate and culture. (SEL Connections)		/7
Total			/49

10. **Student Engagement and Academic Achievement Monitoring:**

Monitor engagement by asking questions and leading discussions, observing participation in collaborative work by seeing how students respond in smaller settings, and polling students using engagement surveys.

Academic achievement should be monitored daily using formative assessments. Good ones for strengthening core instruction may include thumbs-up responses, exit tickets, and quizzes. Biweekly, end-of-unit, and benchmark assessments are metrics your district may have in place for you to use.

11. **Teacher Reflection for Understanding Your Own Impact:**

Following implementation, consider how learning experiences can be improved in future iterations of this project.

Surveying, polling, and student conferences can help improve teaching impact. You might ask questions such as the following:

- *Which classroom activities help you learn most?*

- *What changes do you recommend I make to help you learn better?*

- *What motivates you to learn most?*

- *What can I do better?*

SOURCE: Inspired by GRASP Model by Jay McTighe. By Lifelong Learning Defined, Inc.

APPENDIX C

The Self-Awareness Project and Performance Task Template

Title: The Self-Awareness Project: Connecting Passion to Purpose

Content Area: ELA (Adaptable by Multiple Areas)

Grade Level: 9–12

Duration: 3–3.5 Weeks

1. **Standards to be Assessed** (2–5 standards):	2. **Learning Intentions:**
Identify specific Standards of Learning (<u>CCSS</u> or <u>SOLs</u>) and SEL competencies.	*Student-friendly statements identifying the observable or measurable outcomes desired.*
CCSS.ELA-Literacy.SL.9-10.4: Present information, findings, and supporting evidence clearly, concisely, and logically such that listeners can follow the line of reasoning and the organization, development, substance, and style are appropriate to purpose, audience, and task.	• I can examine and identify my passions and interests following the directions in my 5-step organizer. • I can organize my findings and evidence in my 5-step organizer to support my passion and interests.
CCSS.ELA-Literacy.W.11-12.2: Write informative/explanatory texts to examine and convey complex ideas, concepts, and information clearly and accurately through the effective selection, organization, and analysis of content.	• I can organize my content in my 5-step organizer effectively to ensure clarity and accuracy about solving a problem(s) of practice for a specific person or entity. • I can identify an expert(s) who can mentor and coach me as I build expertise to solve a problem of practice.
SEL Connection(s): Self-awareness, growth mindset, understanding blind spots, asking good questions, seeking assistance, listening to feedback, being open to change, and helping others.	• I can communicate what self-awareness means and how it pertains to making myself happy and fulfilled.
Literacy Connection(s): Reading and writing, analyzing and evaluating text, summarizing and synthesizing information. Writing clear and coherent sentences, using appropriate	• I can build expertise in my passion or interest to solve a problem of practice and develop a model of change framework for others to use to achieve similar success.

(Continued)

(Continued)

grammar, spelling, and punctuation.
Developing ideas and supporting them with
evidence. Organizing and presenting writing
logically and effectively. Speaking and listening,
articulating thoughts and ideas clearly and
effectively, active listening and comprehension,
using gestures, body language, and tone to
enhance communication. Asking questions to
clarify and seek information. Participating in
presentations. Giving and receiving feedback.
Understanding and using nonverbal cues.
Using standard English and appropriate
language for the audience. Adapting speech for
different audiences.

Numeracy Connection(s): Make sense of
problems and persevere in solving them, model
with mathematics, attend to precision, look for
and make use of structure.

- I can write informative/explanatory texts and include mathematical modeling to examine and convey the steps in my framework or model of change.
- I can select appropriate audience members who will benefit most from my presentation information.
- I can develop my presentation to be appropriate for my audience and explain my framework or model of change.
- I can present information clearly and concisely to ensure listeners understand the reasoning behind my findings in my framework or model of change.
- I can use appropriate language and tone in my presentation to engage my audience.

3. **Performance Task Situation or Project Description:**

Young people can live fulfilled lives if they discover what makes them happy and compels them to become the best possible version of themselves. This project allows youth to develop greater self-awareness skills by exploring and connecting their passions and interests to the purpose of making a difference in their communities by helping others. Students begin by brainstorming what makes them happy and compels them to learn and act. They will also identify their passions and interest and identify steps they can take to build expertise in a chosen topic. Mapping their own journey, they will then use what they learn to design a solution for someone or an entity in their community that needs their expertise. To execute their self-awareness project plans, students identify problems of practice and develop a framework of change along with how-to steps they will teach their intended audience to take for its implementation.

4. **Product(s) and/or Performance Task:**

- **Passion to Purpose 5-Step Organizer:** The teacher guides students through discovering their passion (or an interest) and turning it into purpose through various activities. The steps involve the following:
  - Identifying a passion or topic of interest
  - Finding a problem of practice related to your passion or interest
  - Setting a goal to solve the problem of practice and working with experts to develop a solution
  - Creating a framework or model of change to assist others in solving a similar problem of practice in their community

- **Framework or Model of Change:** Students will design an original framework or model of change to organize problem-solving approaches based on their goal(s) and knowledge. The student-developed framework or model must present a visual representation of the theory of the problem, theory of action, and logic model that can guide others with similar pursuits. Additionally, students will map backward from the intended outcomes to highlight necessary elements and details others must know to achieve similar success.

- **Public Presentation:** *Students will, independently or with peers, conduct a public presentation of their framework or model of change. They will do the following:*
  - *Prepare a clear and concise explanation of the problem of practice and the need for a framework or model of change.*
  - *Use visual aids to help represent and illustrate essential elements and components in their framework.*
  - *Present the framework and related steps in a logical and organized manner.*
  - *Demonstrate how the framework can be adapted to help others with similar goals and pursuits achieve success.*
  - *Engage the audience through modeling, explanation, and questions and answers.*

5. Authentic Audience:

Students present their framework or model of change to an audience of their choice, which may include community members (including family members), other youth (e.g., peers, students), industry experts, local politicians, parents, and school and district administrators. The presentation may also include a call to action for the audience to support the project.

6. Student Role(s):

Assuming the role of experts, students will use their developed framework or model of change to:

- Offer support and resources to others with similar interests and pursuits in the community.
- Share their knowledge and expertise in a public forum.
- Coach and mentor those with similar goals to achieve success.

7. Driving Question (DQ):

Since students are exploring their own interests and passions, they will develop their unique DQ. They may work individually or with a peer(s). Here are some DQ sentence starters for them to consider:

- *How do I, as an _____, create _____ about _____? (e.g., "How do I, as an artificial intelligence specialist, develop an AI-powered solution addressing the unique needs of a client?")*
- *How do we, as _____, create _____ about _____? (e.g., "How do we, as artificial intelligence specialists, develop an AI-powered solution addressing the unique needs of a client?")*
- *How can I use _____ to demonstrate _____? (e.g., "How can I use multimedia effectively to demonstrate the role of photosynthesis to plant health?")*
- *How can we use _____ to demonstrate _____? (e.g., "How can we use multimedia effectively to demonstrate the role of photosynthesis to plant health?")*

8a. Alignment Tool for Student Task Instructions and Teaching:

Use the following alignment tool to organize formative assessments and lessons/scaffolds for each learning intention. Also, consider which learning activities align best with the intended standards and outcomes, the completion timeline, and the materials or resources students need. See Table 4.1 in Chapter 4 for a completed example.

(Continued)

(Continued)

PRODUCT(S) AND TASKS	LEARNING INTENTIONS AND PACING	FORMAL AND INFORMAL FORMATIVE ASSESSMENTS	MINI-LESSONS, HIGH-YIELDING STRATEGIES, AND SCAFFOLDS
Passion to Purpose 5-Step Organizer **(3–4 Class Periods)**	I can examine and identify my passions and interests following the directions in my 5-step organizer. (1–2 class periods)	• Written reflection on 5-step organizer • Responses during classroom discussions • Exit ticket	• Teacher-led mini-lesson explaining major concepts • Videos explaining passion and providing service to others • Introduction to *passion to purpose 5-step organizer* • All-class discussion and debrief
	I can organize my findings and evidence in my 5-step organizer to support my passion and interests. (2 class periods)	• Written reflection on 5-step organizer • Feedback protocol using rubric • Checklist • Exit ticket	• Teacher directions and guiding questions • *Passion to purpose 5-step organizer* • Teacher/student feedback
	I can organize my content in my 5-step organizer effectively to ensure clarity and accuracy about solving a problem(s) of practice for a specific person or entity. (1 class period)	• Teacher-led discussion • Written explanation • Feedback protocol using rubric • Checklist • Exit ticket	• Teacher directions and guiding questions • Additional resources pertaining to specific problem(s) • *Passion to purpose 5-step organizer* • Teacher/student feedback

PRODUCT(S) AND TASKS	LEARNING INTENTIONS AND PACING	FORMAL AND INFORMAL FORMATIVE ASSESSMENTS	MINI-LESSONS, HIGH-YIELDING STRATEGIES, AND SCAFFOLDS
	I can identify an expert(s) who can mentor and coach me as I build expertise to solve a problem of practice. (1 class period)	• Written reflection on 5-step organizer • Discussion with teacher • Exit ticket	• Individual and small-group teaching • Additional resources pertaining to specific expert(s) • Teacher/student feedback • *Passion to purpose 5-step organizer*
	I can communicate what self-awareness means and how it pertains to making myself happy and fulfilled. (1 class period)	• Teacher-led discussion • Written and oral explanation • Poster presentation	• Working in pairs • Poster template • Teacher/student feedback • *Passion to purpose 5-step organizer*

9a. Scoring:

Single-point rubric tool for scoring products and performance tasks. See Table 5.1 in Chapter 5 for a completed example.

EMERGING 1–3 PROVIDE FEEDBACK FOR IMPROVEMENT	PROFICIENT 4 GRADE-LEVEL EXPECTATIONS MET PROVIDE FEEDBACK FOR IMPROVEMENT	HIGHLY PROFICIENT 5 PROVIDE FEEDBACK FOR IMPROVEMENT	SCORE
	I can examine and identify my passions and interests following the directions in my 5-step organizer. (W.11-12.2)		/5
	I can organize my findings and evidence in my 5-step organizer to support my passion and interests. (W.11-12.2)		/5

(Continued)

(Continued)

EMERGING 1–3 PROVIDE FEEDBACK FOR IMPROVEMENT	PROFICIENT 4 GRADE-LEVEL EXPECTATIONS MET PROVIDE FEEDBACK FOR IMPROVEMENT	HIGHLY PROFICIENT 5 PROVIDE FEEDBACK FOR IMPROVEMENT	SCORE
	I can organize my content in my 5-step organizer effectively to ensure clarity and accuracy about solving a problem(s) of practice for a specific person or entity. (W.11-12.2)		/5
	I can identify an expert(s) who can mentor and coach me as I build expertise to solve a problem of practice. (W.11-12.2, SL.9-10.4)		/5
	I can communicate what self-awareness means and how it pertains to making myself happy and fulfilled. (W.11-12.2, SL.9-10.4)		/5
Total			/25

8b. **Alignment Tool for Student Task Instructions and Teaching:**

PRODUCT(S) AND TASKS	LEARNING INTENTIONS AND PACING	FORMAL AND INFORMAL FORMATIVE ASSESSMENTS	MINI-LESSONS, HIGH-YIELDING STRATEGIES, AND SCAFFOLDS
Framework or Model of Change (5–7 Class Periods)	I can build expertise in my passion or interest to solve a problem of practice and develop a model of change framework for others to use to achieve similar success. (3 class periods)	• Written reflection • *Framework or model of change* template • Feedback protocol using rubric • Exit ticket	• Teacher-led mini-lesson explaining major concepts • Videos and articles explaining the essential features of a framework or model of change

PRODUCT(S) AND TASKS	LEARNING INTENTIONS AND PACING	FORMAL AND INFORMAL FORMATIVE ASSESSMENTS	MINI-LESSONS, HIGH-YIELDING STRATEGIES, AND SCAFFOLDS
			• Introduction to the *framework or model of change* template • Teacher/student feedback
	I can write informative/explanatory texts and include mathematical modeling to examine and convey the steps in my framework or model of change. (2–3 class periods)	• Descriptive text in the *framework or model of change* template • Feedback protocol using rubric • Checklist • Exit ticket	• Teacher-led mini-lesson explaining mathematical modeling • Resources on mathematical modeling • *Framework or model of change* template • Teacher/student feedback

9b. **Scoring:**

Single-point rubric tool for scoring products and performance tasks. See Table 5.1 in Chapter 5 for a completed example.

EMERGING 1–3 PROVIDE FEEDBACK FOR IMPROVEMENT	PROFICIENT 4 GRADE-LEVEL EXPECTATIONS MET PROVIDE FEEDBACK FOR IMPROVEMENT	HIGHLY PROFICIENT 5 PROVIDE FEEDBACK FOR IMPROVEMENT	SCORE
	I can build expertise in my passion or interest to solve a problem of practice and develop a model of change framework for others to use to achieve similar success. **(W.11-12.2)**		/20

(Continued)

(Continued)

EMERGING 1–3 PROVIDE FEEDBACK FOR IMPROVEMENT	PROFICIENT 4 GRADE-LEVEL EXPECTATIONS MET PROVIDE FEEDBACK FOR IMPROVEMENT	HIGH PROFICIENT 5 PROVIDE FEEDBACK FOR IMPROVEMENT	SCORE
	I can write informative/explanatory texts and include mathematical modeling to examine and convey the steps in my framework or model of change. (W.11-12.2, SL.9-10.4)		/20
Total			/40

8c. **Alignment Tool for Student Task Instructions and Teaching:**

Use the following alignment tool to organize formative assessments and lessons/scaffolds for each learning intention. Also, consider which learning activities align best with the intended standards and outcomes, the completion timeline, and the materials or resources students need. See Table 4.1 in Chapter 4 for a completed example.

PRODUCT(S) AND TASKS	LEARNING INTENTIONS AND PACING	FORMAL AND INFORMAL FORMATIVE ASSESSMENTS	MINI-LESSONS, HIGH-YIELDING STRATEGIES, AND SCAFFOLDS
Public Presentation (3–4 class periods)	I can select appropriate audience members who will benefit most from my presentation information. (1 class period)	• Written notes and reflection • Responses during classroom discussions • Exit ticket	• Teacher-led mini-lesson explaining major concepts • Videos showcasing presentations • All-class discussion and debrief
	I can develop my presentation to be appropriate for my audience and explain my framework or model of change. (3 class periods)	• Feedback protocol using rubric • Presentation checklist • Exit ticket	• Teacher directions and guiding questions • Presentation app (e.g., PowerPoint) • Teacher/student feedback

PRODUCT(S) AND TASKS	LEARNING INTENTIONS AND PACING	FORMAL AND INFORMAL FORMATIVE ASSESSMENTS	MINI-LESSONS, HIGH-YIELDING STRATEGIES, AND SCAFFOLDS
	I can present information clearly and concisely to ensure listeners understand the reasoning behind my findings in my framework or model of change. (3 class periods)	• Teacher-led discussion • Feedback protocol using rubric • Checklist • Exit ticket	• Individual and small-group rehearsal • Additional resources pertaining to presentations • Presentation app • Teacher/student feedback
	I can use appropriate language and tone in my presentation to engage my audience. (3 class periods)	• Written notes • Discussion with teacher	• Individual and small-group rehearsal • Additional resources pertaining to specific expert(s) • Teacher/student feedback

9c. **Scoring:**

Single-point rubric tool for scoring products and performance tasks. See Table 5.1 in Chapter 5 for a completed example.

EMERGING 1–3 PROVIDE FEEDBACK FOR IMPROVEMENT	PROFICIENT 4 GRADE-LEVEL EXPECTATIONS MET PROVIDE FEEDBACK FOR IMPROVEMENT	HIGHLY PROFICIENT 5 PROVIDE FEEDBACK FOR IMPROVEMENT	SCORE
	I can select appropriate audience members who will benefit most from my presentation information. (SL.9-10.4)		/7
	I can develop my presentation to be appropriate for my audience and explain my framework or model of change. (SL.9-10.4, W.11-12.2)		/7

(Continued)

APPENDIX C • THE SELF-AWARENESS PROJECT AND PERFORMANCE TASK TEMPLATE

(Continued)

| | PROFICIENT 4 GRADE-LEVEL EXPECTATIONS MET PROVIDE FEEDBACK FOR IMPROVEMENT | HIGHLY PROFICIENT 5 PROVIDE FEEDBACK FOR IMPROVEMENT | SCORE |
EMERGING 1-3 PROVIDE FEEDBACK FOR IMPROVEMENT			
	I can present information clearly and concisely to ensure listeners understand the reasoning behind my findings in my framework or model of change. (SL.9-10.4, W.11-12.2)		/7
	I can use appropriate language and tone in my presentation to engage my audience. (SL.9-10.4)		/7
Total			/28

10. Student Engagement and Academic Achievement Monitoring:

Monitor engagement by asking questions and leading discussions, observing participation in collaborative work by seeing how students respond in smaller settings, and polling students using engagement surveys.

Academic achievement should be monitored daily using formative assessments. Good ones for strengthening core instruction may include thumbs-up responses, exit tickets, and quizzes. Biweekly, end-of-unit, and benchmark assessments are metrics your district may have in place for you to use.

11. Teacher Reflection for Understanding Your Own Impact:

Following implementation, consider how learning experiences can be improved in future iterations of this project.

Surveying, polling, and student conferences can help improve teaching impact. You might ask questions such as the following:

- *Which classroom activities help you learn most?*
- *What changes do you recommend I make to help you learn better?*
- *What motivates you to learn most?*
- *What can I do better?*

SOURCE: Inspired by GRASP Model by Jay McTighe. By Lifelong Learning Defined, Inc.

APPENDIX D

The Social-Awareness Project and Performance Task Template

Title: The Social-Awareness Project: Improving Our Relationships

Content Area: Visual arts or ELA (Adaptable by Multiple Areas)

Grade Level: 6–12

Duration: 4–5.5 Weeks

1. **Standards to be Assessed** (2–5 standards):	2. **Learning Intentions:**
Identify specific Standards of Learning (CCSS or SOLs) and SEL competencies.	*Student-friendly statements identifying the observable or measurable outcomes desired.*
• **CCSS.ELA-Literacy.W.6-8.3:** Write narratives to develop real or imagined experiences or events using effective technique, well-chosen details, and well-structured event sequences.	• I can write a 500-word personal narrative about my personal experience with empathy and how it impacted me and others at my school.
• **CCSS.ELA-Literacy.W.6-8.3.d:** Use concrete words and phrases and sensory details to convey experiences and events precisely.	• I can write clearly and concisely, referencing essential details of my experience with the benefits of empathy in my narrative.
• **CCSS.ELA-Literacy.W.6-8.3.e:** Provide a conclusion that follows from and reflects on the narrated experiences or events.	• I can use transitions to connect and organize my narrative with a clear start, middle, and conclusion.
• **CCSS.Math.Content.7.G.A.1:** Solve problems involving scale drawings of geometric figures, including computing actual lengths and areas from a scale drawing and reproducing a scale drawing at a different scale.	• I can reflect in my narrative on my experience with empathy and what I learned about the importance of social awareness for building community with others at my school.
• **CCSS.Math.Content.7.RP.A.2:** Recognize and represent proportional relationships between quantities.	• I can identify my classmate or teacher for whom I will create an empathy map.
• **CCSS.Math.Content.MP.1:** Make sense of problems and persevere in solving them.	• I can gather statements from my classmate or teacher that can provide insights into their needs.
• **CCSS.Math.Content.MP.2:** Reason abstractly and quantitatively.	• I can identify and understand the thoughts and feelings that my classmate or teacher might have based on their actions and words.

(Continued)

(Continued)

- **CCSS.Math.Content.MP.4:** Model with mathematics.

- **CCSS.Math.Content.MP.5:** Use appropriate tools strategically.

- **CCSS.Math.Content.MP.6:** Attend to precision.

- **CCSS.Math.Content.MP.7:** Look for and make use of structure.

- *SEL Connection(s): Social awareness includes empathy, understanding the feelings of others, respect, seeking assistance, cultural competence, active listening, teamwork, and seeking to help others.*

- *Literacy Connection(s): Reading and writing, analyzing and evaluating text, summarizing and synthesizing information. Writing clear and coherent sentences, using appropriate grammar, spelling, and punctuation. Developing ideas and supporting them with personal insight. Organizing and presenting a personal narrative using clear and concise language, organization, and reflection.*

- *Numeracy Connection(s): Measurement; using basic geometric shapes and principles to design a mural; proportions, scaling, estimation, and budgeting; and ensuring the mural is symmetrical and balanced.*

- I can identify the challenges that my classmate or teacher might face.

- I can use the empathy map I created to develop more positive outcomes for my classmate or teacher.

- I can determine the size of the surface where the mural will be designed and painted.

- I can measure the different sections of the mural design to ensure accurate proportions and placement.

- I can determine the materials needed for the mural, such as paint, brushes, and other supplies.

- I can track expenses to ensure the project stays within the allotted budget.

- I can use basic geometric shapes and principles like triangles, circles, and lines to create the mural design.

- I can adjust the size of the mural design while maintaining proper proportions and visual appeal.

- I can add my name and one word to the mural describing how I will add value to others in my class and school community.

- I can use symmetry and balance to create visually appealing designs in the mural.

- I can seal the mural to protect it from weather and other forms of damage.

- I can select appropriate audience members who will benefit most from the information presented.

- I can develop my artist statement and talk to be appropriate for my audience and explain the inspiration for the mural.

- I can present information clearly and concisely using photographs or a time-lapse video to ensure the audience understands the mural design process.

- I can use appropriate language and tone to engage my audience.

3. **Performance Task Situation or Project Description:**

Young people are school community members and can improve their social-awareness skills to make a thriving school community for each other and the adults they interact with daily. This project creates space and opportunity for learners to take on the role of change advocates and explore how they can understand other people's feelings and their points of view. They will build empathy to appreciate and respect people different from them, along with learning to follow the rules for interacting appropriately in different social situations at school. They will also learn how to leverage the help from their family and school community by contributing to a class mural. The mural can be painted on a wall or section of the class or school. If painting is not possible, the mural can also be designed and displayed on a bulletin board using paper products. Aspects of this project can also be implemented as a performance task.

4. **Product(s) and/or Performance Task:**

- *Personal Narrative About Empathy:*

  Students compose an original personal narrative of about 500 words defining and detailing their experience with empathy and how it impacted them and others at their school. They may describe an event where empathy was either shown to them or vice versa. The narrative should include individual students' reflections on their personal experiences with the benefits of empathy. The narrative should also provide the following:

  - *Adherence to good grammar and sentence structure*
  - *Clear organization with a start, middle, and end*
  - *Takeaways on the importance of social awareness for building a positive and safe school community*

- *Empathy Map:*

  Students will create an empathy map as a helpful tool for being kind and connecting better with others by understanding better how they may feel. They may choose another classmate or a teacher as the subject of their map. To create their empathy map, students will observe what the other person says and does and then imagine themselves as that person and think about what they might think and feel.

- *Mural Design and Public Unveiling:*

  Students will work with their teacher, classmates, and other adults to design a mural to showcase everyone in the class's name and one word to describe how they will add value to each other and the overall school community. They will do the following:

  - *Identify a wall or space to design the mural in their classroom or school. They can decide to either paint the mural or use paper products.*
  - *Use basic geometric shapes and principles to create the mural design.*
  - *Adjust the size of the mural design while maintaining proper proportions and visual appeal.*
  - *Determine the materials needed for the mural and remain within a budget.*
  - *Create a compelling artistic presentation using technology.*

5. **Authentic Audience:**

Students unveil their mural design to an audience of their choice, which may include community members (including family members), other youth (e.g., peers, students), industry experts, local politicians, parents, and school and district administrators. The presentation may also include a call to action for the audience to support the project.

6. **Student Role(s):**

Assuming the role of change advocates and artists, students will use their mural design to:

- Provide empathy to classmates and teachers by understanding how they feel.
- Offer support and resources to others in their class and wider school community.
- Share their knowledge and expertise in a public forum.

7. **Driving Question (DQ):**

Since students are improving their own social awareness and in community with others, there will be two DQs for the project. For one DQ, they answer will independently, and for the other, they will answer with their classmates.

- *How do I improve my social-awareness skills to understand better how others feel and to see their point of view?*
- *How does our class, as part of the larger school community, create a mural representing each unique individual and how they can add value to others?*

(Continued)

(Continued)

8a. **Alignment Tool for Student Task Instructions and Teaching:**

Use the following alignment tool to organize formative assessments and lessons/scaffolds for each learning intention. Also, consider which learning activities align best with the intended standards and outcomes, the completion timeline, and the materials or resources students need. See Table 4.1 for a completed example.

FINAL PRODUCT	LEARNING INTENTIONS AND PACING	FORMAL AND INFORMAL FORMATIVE ASSESSMENTS	MINI-LESSONS, HIGH-YIELDING STRATEGIES, AND SCAFFOLDS
Personal Narrative (3–4 Class Periods)	I can write a 500-word personal narrative about my personal experience with empathy and how it impacted me and others at my school. (3–4 class periods)	• Brainstorm ideas in graphic organizer • Personal narrative draft 1 • Responses during classroom discussions • Exit ticket	• Teacher-led mini-lesson explaining major concepts • Teacher modeling personal narrative • Graphic organizer to organize thoughts and ideas • All-class discussion and debrief
	I can write clearly and concisely, referencing essential details of my experience with the benefits of empathy in my narrative. (3 class periods)	• Draft 1 feedback protocol using rubric • Update graphic organizer reflect and revise • Exit ticket	• Teacher-led empathy-building activity • Graphic organizer • Teacher/student feedback • Whole-class reflection
	I can use transitions to connect and organize my narrative with a clear start, middle, and conclusion. (3 class periods)	• Teacher-led discussion • Begin draft 2 • Feedback protocol using rubric • Update graphic organizer • Exit ticket	• Mini-lesson on transitions • Individual and small-group teaching • Graphic organizer • Teacher/student feedback
	I can reflect in my narrative on my experience with empathy and what I learned about the importance of social-awareness for building community with others at my school. (1 class period)	• Begin draft 3 • Update graphic organizer • Discussion with teacher • Exit ticket	• Individual and small-group teaching • Additional resources pertaining to grammar and sentence structure • Teacher/student feedback • Graphic organizer

9a. **Scoring:**

Single-point rubric tool for scoring products and performance tasks. See Table 5.1 for a completed example.

EMERGING 1–3 PROVIDE FEEDBACK FOR IMPROVEMENT	PROFICIENT 4 GRADE-LEVEL EXPECTATIONS MET PROVIDE FEEDBACK FOR IMPROVEMENT	HIGHLY PROFICIENT 5 PROVIDE FEEDBACK FOR IMPROVEMENT	SCORE
	I can write a 500-word personal narrative about my personal experience with empathy and how it impacted me and others at my school. (W.6-8.3, W.6-8.3.e)		/7.5
	I can write clearly and concisely, referencing essential details of my experience with the benefits of empathy in my narrative. (W.6-8.3)		/7.5
	I can use transitions to connect and organize my narrative with a clear start, middle, and conclusion. (W.6-8.3, W.6-8.3.d)		/7.5
	I can reflect in my narrative on my experience with empathy and what I learned about the importance of social awareness for building community with others at my school. (W.6-8.3.e)		/7.5
Total			/30

(Continued)

(Continued)

8b. Alignment Tool for Student Task Instructions and Teaching:

FINAL PRODUCT	LEARNING INTENTIONS AND PACING	FORMAL AND INFORMAL FORMATIVE ASSESSMENTS	MINI-LESSONS, HIGH-YIELDING STRATEGIES, AND SCAFFOLDS
Empathy Map (3 Class Periods)	I can identify my classmate or teacher for whom I will create an empathy map. (1 class period)	• Brainstorm ideas • Begin developing empathy map • Responses during classroom discussions • Exit ticket	• Teacher-led mini-lesson explaining major concepts • Teacher modeling empathy map development • Empathy map template • All-class discussion and debrief
	I can gather statements from my classmate or teacher that can provide insights into their needs. (2 class periods)	• Feedback protocol using rubric • Update empathy map • Reflect and revise • Exit ticket	• Teacher-led empathy building activity • Empathy map template • Teacher/student feedback • Whole-class reflection
	I can identify and understand the thoughts and feelings that my classmate or teacher might have based on their actions and words. (2 class periods)	• Teacher-led discussion • Update empathy map • Reflect and revise • Exit ticket	• Mini-lesson on empathy • Individual and small-group teaching • Empathy map template • Teacher/student feedback
	I can identify the challenges that my classmate or teacher might face. (1 class period)	• Update empathy map • Feedback protocol using rubric • Discussion with teacher • Exit ticket	• Individual and small-group teaching • Additional resources pertaining to using empathy maps • Empathy map template • Teacher/student feedback
	I can use the empathy map I created to develop more positive outcomes for my classmate or teacher. (1 class period)	• Personal reflection • Responses during classroom discussions • Exit ticket	• Individual and small-group teaching • Additional resources pertaining to using empathy maps • Empathy map template • Teacher/student feedback

9b. **Scoring:**

Single-point rubric tool for scoring products and performance tasks. See Table 5.1 for a completed example.

EMERGING 1–3 PROVIDE FEEDBACK FOR IMPROVEMENT	PROFICIENT 4 GRADE-LEVEL EXPECTATIONS MET PROVIDE FEEDBACK FOR IMPROVEMENT	HIGHLY PROFICIENT 5 PROVIDE FEEDBACK FOR IMPROVEMENT	SCORE
	I can identify my classmate or teacher for whom I will create an empathy map. (Social-Awareness Competency)		/2.5
	I can gather statements from my classmate or teacher that can provide insights into their needs. (Active Listening and Literacy Connections)		/2.5
	I can identify and understand the thoughts and feelings that my classmate or teacher might have based on their actions and words. (Empathy and Literacy Connections)		/2.5
	I can identify the challenges that my classmate or teacher might face. (Empathy and SEL Connections)		/2.5
	I can use the empathy map I created to develop more positive outcomes for my classmate or teacher. (Empathy and SEL Connections)		/2.5
Total			/12.5

(Continued)

(Continued)

8c. Alignment Tool for Student Task Instructions and Teaching:

Use the following alignment tool to organize formative assessments and lessons/scaffolds for each learning intention. Also, consider which learning activities align best with the intended standards and outcomes, the completion timeline, and the materials or resources students need. See Table 4.1 for a completed example.

FINAL PRODUCT	LEARNING INTENTIONS AND PACING	FORMAL AND INFORMAL FORMATIVE ASSESSMENTS	MINI-LESSONS, HIGH-YIELDING STRATEGIES, AND SCAFFOLDS
Mural Design (7–8 class periods)	• I can determine the size of the surface where the mural will be designed and painted. • I can measure the different sections of the mural design to ensure accurate proportions and placement. (2–3 class periods)	• Brainstorm ideas and sketch the design • Space measurement • Responses during classroom discussions • Exit ticket	• Teacher-led mini-lesson on measurement, proportions, and placement for mural • Teacher modeling • All-class discussion and debrief
	• I can determine the materials needed for the mural, such as paint, brushes, and other supplies. • I can track expenses to ensure the project stays within the allotted budget. (1 class period)	• Materials list development and checklist • Updating budget spreadsheet • Responses during classroom discussions • Exit ticket	• Teacher-led mini-lesson on materials and budgeting • Budget spreadsheet template • Teacher/student feedback • Whole-class reflection
	• I can use basic geometric shapes and principles like triangles, circles, and lines to create the mural design. • I can adjust the size of the mural design while maintaining proper proportions and visual appeal. (3–4 class periods)	• Sketch the details using geometric shapes • Checking for proper proportions and visual appeal • Reflect and revise • Exit ticket	• Mini-lesson on using geometric shapes in art • Individual and small-group teaching • Critique with an expert (proper proportions and visual appeal) • Teacher/student feedback

FINAL PRODUCT	LEARNING INTENTIONS AND PACING	FORMAL AND INFORMAL FORMATIVE ASSESSMENTS	MINI-LESSONS, HIGH-YIELDING STRATEGIES, AND SCAFFOLDS
	• I can add my name and one word to the mural describing how I will add value to others in my class and school community. • I can use symmetry and balance to create visually appealing designs in the mural. • I can seal the mural to protect it from weather and other forms of damage. (5–6 class periods)	• Sketch and paint the details • Reflect and revise • Add finishing touches • Seal the mural • Exit ticket	• Teacher-led mini-lesson on symmetry and balance • Individual and small-group teaching • Critique with an expert • Empathy map template • Teacher/student feedback
Public Unveiling (2–3 class periods)	I can select appropriate audience members who will benefit most from the information presented. (1 class period)	• Written notes and reflection • Responses during classroom discussions • Exit ticket	• Teacher-led mini-lesson explaining major concepts • Videos showcasing presentations • All-class discussion and debrief
	I can develop my artist statement and talk to be appropriate for my audience and explain the inspiration for the mural. (2–3 class periods)	• Feedback protocol using rubric • Presentation checklist • Exit ticket	• Teacher directions and guiding questions • Presentation app (e.g., PowerPoint) • Teacher/student feedback
	I can present information clearly and concisely using photographs or a time-lapse video to ensure the audience understands the mural design process. (2–3 class periods)	• Teacher-led discussion • Time-lapse video editing • Photo journal development • Feedback protocol using rubric • Checklist • Exit ticket	• Individual and small-group rehearsal • Additional resources pertaining to presentations • Presentation app • Teacher/student feedback

(Continued)

(Continued)

FINAL PRODUCT	LEARNING INTENTIONS AND PACING	FORMAL AND INFORMAL FORMATIVE ASSESSMENTS	MINI-LESSONS, HIGH-YIELDING STRATEGIES, AND SCAFFOLDS
	I can use appropriate language and tone in my presentation to engage my audience. (3 class periods)	• Written notes • Discussion with teacher	• Individual and small-group rehearsal • Additional resources pertaining to specific expert(s) • Teacher/student feedback

9c. **Scoring:**

Single-point rubric tool for scoring products and performance tasks. See Table 5.1 for a completed example.

EMERGING 1–3 PROVIDE FEEDBACK FOR IMPROVEMENT	PROFICIENT 4 GRADE-LEVEL EXPECTATIONS MET PROVIDE FEEDBACK FOR IMPROVEMENT	HIGHLY PROFICIENT 5 PROVIDE FEEDBACK FOR IMPROVEMENT	SCORE
	• I can determine the size of the surface where the mural will be designed and painted. • I can measure the different sections of the mural design to ensure accurate proportions and placement. (7.G.A.1, 7.RP.A.2)		/6
	• I can determine the materials needed for the mural, such as paint, brushes, and other supplies. • I can track expenses to ensure the project stays within the allotted budget. (MP.5 and Numeracy Connections)		/6

EMERGING 1–3 PROVIDE FEEDBACK FOR IMPROVEMENT	PROFICIENT 4 GRADE-LEVEL EXPECTATIONS MET PROVIDE FEEDBACK FOR IMPROVEMENT	HIGHLY PROFICIENT 5 PROVIDE FEEDBACK FOR IMPROVEMENT	SCORE
	• I can use basic geometric shapes and principles like triangles, circles, and lines to create the mural design. • I can adjust the size of the mural design while maintaining proper proportions and visual appeal. (7.G.A.1, 7.RP.A.2)		/6
	• I can add my name and one word to the mural describing how I will add value to others in my class and school community. • I can use symmetry and balance to create visually appealing designs in the mural. • I can seal the mural to protect it from weather and other forms of damage. (7.G.A.1, 7.RP.A.2)		/6
	I can select appropriate audience members who will benefit most from the information presented. (SL.9-10.4)		/6
	I can develop my artist statement and talk to be appropriate for my audience and explain the inspiration for the mural. (SL.9-10.4, W.11-12.2)		/6

(Continued)

EMERGING 1–3 PROVIDE FEEDBACK FOR IMPROVEMENT	PROFICIENT 4 GRADE-LEVEL EXPECTATIONS MET PROVIDE FEEDBACK FOR IMPROVEMENT	HIGHLY PROFICIENT 5 PROVIDE FEEDBACK FOR IMPROVEMENT	SCORE
	I can present information clearly and concisely using photographs or a time-lapse video to ensure the audience understands the mural design process. (SL.9-10.4, W.11-12.2)		/6
	I can use appropriate language and tone in my presentation to engage my audience. (SL.9-10.4)		/6
Total			/48

10. Student Engagement and Academic Achievement Monitoring:

Monitor engagement by asking questions and leading discussions, observing participation in collaborative work by seeing how students respond in smaller settings, and polling students using engagement surveys.

Academic achievement should be monitored daily using formative assessments. Good ones for strengthening core instruction may include thumbs-up responses, exit tickets, and quizzes. Biweekly, end-of-unit, and benchmark assessments are metrics your district may have in place for you to use.

11. Teacher Reflection for Understanding Your Own Impact:

Following implementation, consider how learning experiences can be improved in future iterations of this project.

Surveying, polling, and student conferences can help improve teaching impact. You might ask questions such as the following:

- *Which classroom activities help you learn most?*
- *What changes do you recommend I make to help you learn better?*
- *What motivates you to learn most?*
- *What can I do better?*

SOURCE: Inspired by GRASP Model by Jay McTighe. By Lifelong Learning Defined, Inc.

REFERENCES
AND RESOURCES

Adams-Stafford, S. (2019). *How to make the most out of experts when you involve them in projects.* Retrieved July 18, 2022, from https://www.pblworks.org/blog/how-make-most-out-experts-when-you-involve-them-projects

Ahmed, N. (2021). *Client management: A guide to winning and retaining clients (expert tips).* Retrieved July 20, 2022, from https://www.cloudways.com/blog/client-management/

ASCD. (n.d.). *Jay Mctighe.* Retrieved November 3, 2022, from https://www.ascd.org/people/jay-mctighe

Baines, A. M., De Vivo, K., Warner, N., DeBarger, A., Udall, D., Zuckerbrod, N., & Felsen, K. (2021). *Why social and emotional learning is essential to project-based learning.* Retrieved July 20, 2022, from https://www.lucasedresearch.org/wp-content/uploads/2021/02/SEL-White-Paper.pdf

Barkley, S. (2019, February 10). *The impact of knowing and being known.* Retrieved October 3, 2022, from barkleypd.com/blog/knowing-your-students

Barrington, K. (2022). *The 15 biggest failures of the American public education system.* Retrieved July 20, 2022, from https://www.publicschoolreview.com/blog/the-15-biggest-failures-of-the-american-public-education-system

Bland, D. (2020). What is an empathy map? Retrieved April 28, 2023, from https://www.accenture.com/us-en/blogs/software-engineering-blog/what-is-an-empathy-map

Bowen, M. (2021). *Strong core instruction: What it is and how it can address inequity and achievement gaps.* Retrieved October 21, 2022, from https://www.learningsciences.com/blog/core-instruction-improve/

Bruyckere, P. (2019). *From experience to meaning: The update list of effect sizes by John Hattie, but. . . .* Retrieved November 6, 2022, from https://theeconomyofmeaning.com/2019/11/11/the-update-list-of-effect-sizes-by-john-hattie-but/

Cal State East Bay. (2022). *Self care: Lessons learned after two years of the pandemic.* Retrieved July 20, 2022, from https://www.csueastbay.edu/news-center/2022/03/self-care-lessons-learned-after-two-years-of-the-pandemic.html

Campellone, J., & Turley, R. K. (2021). *Understanding the teen brain.* University of Rochester Medical Center Health Encyclopedia. Retrieved February 20, 2023, from www.urmc.rochester.edu/encyclopedia/content%20.aspx?contenttypeid=1&contentid=3051

Cavell, T. (2004). *Valuing emotions.* Retrieved July 2, 2023, from https://www.psychomedia.it/rapaport-klein/cavell04.htm

Center for Excellence in Teaching and Learning. (n.d.). *The one-minute paper.* Retrieved July 19, 2022, from https://www.rochester.edu/college/cetl/faculty/one-minute-paper.html

Centers for Disease Control and Prevention (CDC). (2021). *New CDC data illuminate youth mental health threats during the COVID-19 pandemic.* Retrieved July 21, 2022, from https://www.cdc.gov/media/releases/2022/p0331-youth-mental-health-covid-19.html

Cherry, K. (2022, February 25). *Emotions and types of emotional responses: The three key elements that make up emotion.* Retrieved August 3, 2022, from http://www.verywell mind.com/what-are-emotions-2795178

Christensen Institute. (2021). *Fall 2021 fact sheet.* Retrieved May 5, 2023, from https://www.christenseninstitute.org/wp-content/uploads/2021/12/Fall-2021-Fact-Sheet.pdf

Cohen, R. K., Opatosky, D. K., Savage, J., Stevens, S. O., & Darrah, E. P. (2021). *The metacognitive student: How to teach academic, social, and emotional intelligence in every content area.* Solution Tree Press.

Colburn, L., & Beggs, L. (2021). *The wraparound guide: How to gather student voice, build community partnerships, and cultivate hope.* Solution Tree Press.

Collaborative for Academic, Social, and Emotional Learning (CASEL). (2021). *The CASEL guide to schoolwide social and emotional learning.* Retrieved July 28, 2022, from https://schoolguide.casel.org/resource/the-casel-guide-to-schoolwide-sel-essentials/

Collaborative for Academic, Social, and Emotional Learning (CASEL). (n.d.-a.). *What does the research say?* Retrieved July 28, 2022, from https://casel.org/fundamentals-of-sel/what-does-the-research-say/

Collaborative for Academic, Social, and Emotional Learning (CASEL). (n.d.-b.). *What is the CASEL framework?* Retrieved July 28, 2022, from https://casel.org/fundamentals-of-sel/what-is-the-casel-framework/

Complete Dissertation. (n.d.). *Effect size.* Retrieved November 11, 2022, from https://www.statisticssolutions.com/free-resources/directory-of-statistical-analyses/effect-size/

Corwin. (n.d.-a). *Guidelines for writing learning intentions and success criteria.* Retrieved June 17, 2023, from https://resources.corwin.com/sites/default/files/06.6_Guidelines%20for%20Writing%20LI%20%26%20SC.pdf

Corwin. (n.d.-b). *The visible learning research.* Retrieved October 28, 2022, from https://us.corwin.com/en-us/nam/the-visible-learning-research

Covey, S. R. (2020). *The 7 habits of highly effective people: Powerful lessons in personal change* (30th anniversary edition). Simon & Schuster.

Cuemath. (n.d.). *Average.* Retrieved October 25, 2022, from https://www.cuemath.com/data/average/

Dacey, L., & Eston, R. (2003). *Collecting, representing and interpreting data.* Retrieved October 25, 2022, from https://mathsolutions.com/ms_classroom_lessons/collecting-representing-interpreting-data/

Defined Learning. (2015). *What is a performance task (part 1)?* Retrieved October 31, 2022, from https://blog.performancetask.com/what-is-a-performance-task-part-1-9fa0d99ead3b

Defined Learning. (n.d.). *Performance tasks.* Retrieved October 31, 2022, from https://www.definedlearning.com/pd-center/performance-tasks/

Deutscher, R. R., Holthuis, N. C., Maldonado, S. I., Pecheone, R. L., Schultz, S. E., Wei, R. C., & Lucas Education Research. (2021). *Project-based learning leads to gains in science and other subjects in middle school and benefits all learners.* Lucas Education Research.

DeVito, M. (2016). *Factors influencing student engagement* [Certificate of Advanced Study Thesis]. Sacred Heart University. http://digitalcommons.sacredheart.edu/edl/11

Dewey, J. (1933). *How we think: A restatement of the relation of reflective thinking to the educative process.* Henry Regnery.

Dorn, E., Hancock, B., Sarakatsannis, J., & Viruleg, E. (2020). *COVID-19 and learning loss—Disparities grow and students need help.* Retrieved July 10, 2022, from https://www.mckinsey.com/industries/public-and-social-sector/our-insights/covid-19-and-learning-loss-disparities-grow-and-students-need-help

Duke, N. K., Halvorsen, A.-L., Strachan, S. L., Kim, J., & Konstantopoulos, S. (2020). Putting PjBL to the test: The impact of project-based learning on second graders' social studies and literacy learning and motivation in low-SES school settings. *American Educational Research Journal, 58*(1).

Durlak, J. A., Weissberg, R. P., Dymnicki, A. B., Taylor, R. D., & Schellinger, K. B. (2011). The impact of enhancing students' social and emotional learning: A meta-analysis of school-based universal interventions. *Child Development, 82*(1), 405–432.

Dyer, K. (2015). *Research proof points: Better student engagement improves student learning.* Retrieved October 29, 2022, from https://www.nwea.org/blog/2015/research-proof-points-better-student-engagement-improves-student-learning/

Edsys. (2018). *15 best pedagogical strategies for innovative learning.* Retrieved October 21, 2022, from https://www.edsys.in/best-pedagogical-strategies/

Edutopia. (2015). *Gaining understanding of what your students know.* Retrieved October 30, 2022, from https://www.edutopia.org/practice/exit-tickets-checking-understanding

Edutopia. (2016). *Critique protocol: Helping students produce high-quality work.* Retrieved July 19, 2022, from https://www.edutopia.org/video/critique-protocol-helping-students-produce-high-quality-work

Edutopia. (2019a). *Inviting participation with thumbs-up responses.* Retrieved October 30, 2022, from https://www.edutopia.org/video/inviting-participation-thumbs-responses

Edutopia. (2019b). *60-second strategy: TAG feedback.* Retrieved November 7, 2022, from https://www.edutopia.org/video/60-second-strategy-tag-feedback

Einstein, A. (2010). *The ultimate quotable Einstein.* Princeton University Press.

Eisenberg, N., Smith, C. L., & Spinrad, T. L. (2010). Effortful control: Relations with emotion regulation, adjustment, and socialization in childhood. *Child Development*, *81*(1), 128–137. https://doi.org/10.1111/j.1467-8624.2009.01397.x

EL Education. (2013). *Say something protocol.* Retrieved December 17, 2022, from https://cdn5-ss14.sharpschool.com/UserFiles/Servers/Server_917767/File/Programs%20&%20Services/Professional%20Development/PBL/22%20Say%20Something.pdf

EL Education. (n.d.-a). *Collaborative culture: Protocols.* Retrieved December 17, 2022, from https://eleducation.org/resources/collaborative-culture-protocols

EL Education. (n.d.-b). *Critique protocol.* Retrieved November 7, 2022, from https://eleducation.org/resources/critique-protocol

Emerich France, P. (2020). *Using the workshop model to foster independence.* Retrieved November 6, 2022, from https://www.edutopia.org/article/using-workshop-model-foster-independence

Eric. (2022). *What is adaptive gaming? (everything you need to know).* Retrieved November 18, 2022, from https://streamersplaybook.com/what-is-adaptive-gaming-everything-you-need-to-know

Fisher, J. (2018). Prefrontal cortex: The science of psychotherapy. *The Science of Psychotherapy.* Retrieved February 20, 2023, from https://www.thescienceofpsychotherapy.com/prefrontal-cortex/

Formplus. (n.d.). *Formal vs. informal assessment: 15 key differences & similarities.* Retrieved November 1, 2022, from https://www.formpl.us/blog/formal-vs-informal-assessment

Fort Bend Taekwondo. (2019). *Endorphins—The key to effort and focus in children and teens.* Retrieved November 14, 2022, from https://fortbendtkd.com/2019/05/07/thekeytoeffort

Fritscher, L. (2023). *The psychology of fear.* Retrieved April 29, 2023, from https://www.verywellmind.com/the-psychology-of-fear-2671696

Fuligni, A., & Galván, A. (2022). *Young people need experiences that boost their mental health.* Retrieved January 13, 2023, from https://www.nature.com/articles/d41586-022-03172-y

Garmston, R., & Wellman, B. (2009). *The adaptive school: A sourcebook for developing collaborative groups* (2nd ed.). Christopher-Gordon.

Glossary of Education Reform. (2013). *Formative assessment.* Retrieved November 10, 2022, from https://www.edglossary.org/formative-assessment/

Glossary of Education Reform. (2014). *Summative assessment.* Retrieved November 10, 2022, from https://www.edglossary.org/summative-assessment/

Grand Canyon University. (2022). *What is scaffolding in education?* Retrieved December 20, 2022, from https://www.gcu.edu/blog/teaching-school-administration/what-scaffolding-education

Gray, A. (n.d.). *Constructivist teaching and learning* (SSTA Research Centre Report #97-07). Retrieved July 10, 2022, from https://saskschoolboards.ca/wp-content/uploads/97-07.htm#EXECUTIVE%20SUMMARY

Gray, D., Brown, S., & Macanufo, J. (2010). *Gamestorming: A playbook for innovators, rulebreakers, and changemakers*. O'Reilly.

Greater Good Magazine. (n.d.). *What is empathy?* Retrieved September 8, 2022, from https://greatergood.berkeley.edu/topic/empathy/definition

Groshell, Z. (n.d.). *What is instructional design and does it matter for K–12 education?* Retrieved October 21, 2022, from https://educationrickshaw.com/2019/10/21/what-is-instructional-design-and-does-it-matter-for-k-12-education

Gross, J. J. (1998). Sharpening the focus: Emotion regulation, arousal, and social competence. *Psychological Inquiry*, 9, 287–290. https://doi.org/10.1207/s15327965pli0904_8

Gross, J. J. (2015). The extended process model of emotion regulation: Elaborations, applications, and future directions. *Psychological Inquiry*, 26(1), 130–137. https://doi.org/10.1080/1047840X.2015 .989751

Groundwork USA. (n.d.). *What is an asset? Examples and definitions*. Retrieved October 21, 2022, from https://groundworkusa.org/eqdevtools/asset-examples/

Harvard Business Publishing. (2022). *Why your students are disengaged*. Retrieved November 11, 2022, from https://hbsp .harvard.edu/inspiring-minds/why-your -students-are-disengaged

Haskell, J. (2013). *Working agreements*. Retrieved December 14, 2022, from https://www.uvm.edu/sites/default/files/working -agreements-defined.pdf

Hattie, J. (2009). *Visible learning: A synthesis of over 800 meta-analyses related to achievement*. Routledge.

Heick, T. (n.d.). *Sentence stems for higher-level conversation in the classroom*. Retrieved December 17, 2022, from https://www.teach-thought.com/critical-thinking/sentence -stems/

Hinton, J. (2021). *Why knowledge of students is important for effective teaching*. Retrieved October 3, 2022, from https://www.jeffreya hinton.com/post/why-knowledge-of-stu dents-is-important-for-effective-teaching

Houser, K. (n.d.). *8 strategies for scaffolding instruction*. Retrieved November 4, 2022, from https://www.mshouser.com/teaching-tips/8-strate gies-for-scaffolding-instruction

Hurst, B., Wallace, R., & Nixon, S. B. (2013). The impact of social interaction on student learning. *Reading Horizons: A Journal of Literacy and Language Arts*, 52(4), https://scholarworks.wmich.edu/reading_horizons/vol52/iss4/5

Hurst, S. (2014). *What is the difference between RTI and MTSS?* Retrieved October 25, 2022, from https://readinghorizons.website/blog/what-is-the-difference-between-rti-and-mtss

Kenrick, D. T., Griskevicius, V., Neuberg, S. L., & Schaller, M. (2010). Renovating the pyramid of needs: Contemporary extensions built upon ancient foundations. *Perspectives on Psychological Science*, 5(3), 292–314. https://doi.org/10.1177/1745691610369469

Krajcik, J., Schneider, B., Miller, E., Chen, I. C., Bradford, L., Bartz, K., & Lucas Education Research. (2021). *Project-based learning increases science achievement in elementary schools and improves social and emotional learning*. Lucas Education Research.

Kurtz, H. (2022). *A profession in crisis: Findings from a national teacher survey*. Retrieved July 10, 2022, from https://www.edweek .org/research-center/reports/teaching-pro fession-in-crisis-national-teacher-survey

LaVogue, T. (2020). *Why I scrum: Using a project management tool for PBL*. Retrieved July 19, 2022, from https://www.pblworks .org/blog/why-i-scrum-using-project-man agement-tool-pbl

Learning Focused. (n.d.). *High yield instructional strategies 101: Exemplary schools focus on high yield instructional strategies*. Retrieved October 25, 2022, from https://learningfo cused.com/high-yield-instructional-strategies

Lucas Education Research (LER). (2021). *Rigorous project-based learning is a powerful lever for improving equity*. Retrieved July 10, 2022, from https://www.lucasedresearch .org/research/research-briefs/

Lucas Education Research (LER). (n.d.-a). *Core practices for project-based teaching*. Retrieved July 2, 2023, from https://www.lucasedresearch.org/grat-awards/core-practices-for-project-based-teaching/

Lucas Education Research (LER). (n.d.-b). *What guides our work*. Retrieved July 10, 2022, from https://www.lucasedresearch .org/mission/

Lynette, R., & Noack, C. (n.d.). *The workshop model: Tips and strategies for your classroom.* Retrieved April 29, 2023, from https://minds-in-bloom.com/the-workshop-model-tips-and-strategies/

Magnify Learning. (n.d.). *What is an entry event in PBL?* Retrieved November 18, 2022, from https://www.magnifylearningin.org/entry-events

Mahoney, J., Durlak, J., & Weissberg, R. (2018). *An update on social and emotional learning outcome research.* Retrieved August 1, 2022, from kappanonline.org/social-emotional-learning-outcome-research-mahoney-durlak-weissberg/

Mason, J. (2021). *We are teaching through trauma.* Retrieved July 11, 2022, from https://www.weareteachers.com/teaching-through-trauma/

May, T. (2021). *The empathy map: A human-centered tool for understanding how your audience thinks.* Retrieved September 8, 2022, from https://xplane.com/the-empathy-map-a-human-centered-tool-for-understanding-how-your-audience-thinks/

Mentally Healthy Schools. (n.d.). *Emotion wheel.* Retrieved August 6, 2022, from https://www.mentallyhealthyschools.org.uk/media/2001/emotion-wheel.pdf

Mergendoller, J. (2018). *Defining high quality PBL: A look at the research.* Retrieved July 19, 2022, from https://hqpbl.org/wp-content/uploads/2018/04/Defining-High-Quality-PBL-A-Look-at-the-Research-.pdf

Merrill, S. (2019). *How-to: The jigsaw method, revisited.* Retrieved October 25, 2022, from https://www.edutopia.org/article/how-jigsaw-method-revisited

Metcalf, T. (n.d.). *What's your plan? Accurate decision making within a multi-tier system of supports: Critical areas in tier 1.* Retrieved October 25, 2022, from http://www.rtinetwork.org/essential/tieredinstruction/tier1/accurate-decision-making-within-a-multi-tier-system-of-supports-critical-areas-in-tier-1

Meyer, C. (2012). Emotions vs. feelings. *The Emotional Detective.* Retrieved April 29, 2023, from https://emotionaldetective.typepad.com/emotional-detective/2012/04/emotions-vs-feelings.html

National Association of Secondary School Principals. (2022). *School safety survey.* Retrieved February 24, 2023, from https://survey.nassp.org/2022/#safety

National Center for Education Statistics. (2021). *The condition of education 2021.* Retrieved February 24, 2023, from https://nces.ed.gov/programs/coe/

National Geographic. (n.d.). *Cultural identity.* Retrieved October 3, 2022, from https://education.nationalgeographic.org/resource/resource-library-cultural-identity

National School Reform Faculty (NSRF). (n.d.). *Critical friends groups purpose of work.* Retrieved November 7, 2022, from https://www.nsrfharmony.org/wp-content/uploads/2017/10/cfg_purpose_work_0.pdf

NCTE. (n.d.). *Brainstorming and reviewing using the carousel strategy.* Retrieved December 20, 2022, from https://www.readwritethink.org/professional-development/strategy-guides/brainstorming-reviewing-using-carousel

PBLWorks. (2022). *PBL world 2022.* Retrieved July 19, 2022, from https://www.pblworks.org/pbl-world-2022

PBS Kids. (n.d.). *Design Squad global.* Retrieved May 1, 2023, from https://pbskids.org/designsquad/

Peanut Butter Fish Lessons. (n.d.). *Four number relationships children need to learn.* Retrieved October 25, 2022, from https://peanutbutterfishlessons.com/four-number-relationships/

Peixoto, J. M., & Moura, E. P. (2020). Health empathy map: Creation of an instrument for empathy development. *Revista Brasileira de Educação Médica,* 44(1), Article e029. https://doi.org/10.1590/1981-5271v44.1-20190151.ing

Pivot. (n.d.). *The role of evaluation and reflection in teaching and school improvement.* Retrieved November 6, 2022, from https://pivotpl.com/the-role-of-evaluation-and-reflection-in-teaching-and-school-improvement/

Plutchik, R. (2001). The nature of emotions: Human emotions have deep evolutionary roots, a fact that may explain their complexity and provide tools for clinical practice. *American Scientist,* 89(4), 344–350.

Poll Everywhere. (n.d.). *Are your students actually learning? How to effectively measure student engagement*. Retrieved October 25, 2022, from https://blog.polleverywhere.com/how-to-effectively-measure-student-engagement/

Professional Learning Supports. (2014). *John Hattie: Know thy impact*. Retrieved October 30, 2022, from https://vimeo.com/88176199

Psychology. (n.d.). *Communal relationships*. Retrieved December 14, 2022, from http://psychology.iresearchnet.com/social-psychology/interpersonal-relationships/communal-relationships/

QuestionPro. (n.d.). *Top 16 student survey questions to enhance your student feedback*. Retrieved October 30, 2022, from https://www.questionpro.com/blog/student-survey/

Rigoni, B., & Nelson, B. (2016). *Do employees really know what's expected of them?* Retrieved December 14, 2022, from https://news.gallup.com/businessjournal/195803/employees-really-know-expected.aspx?g_source=WWWV7HP&g_medium=topic&g_campaign=tiles

Rochester, N. (2019). *Design thinking finds its place in project management*. Retrieved July 19, 2022, from https://blog.adobe.com/en/publish/2019/11/18/design-thinking-finds-its-place-in-project-management#gs.kmz56l

Saavedra, A. R., Liu, Y., Haderlein, S. K., Rapaport, A., Garland, M., Hoepfner, D., & Lucas Education Research. (2021). *Project-based learning boosts student achievement in AP courses*. Lucas Education Research.

School Reform Initiative (SRI). (2017). *Charrette protocol*. Retrieved November 7, 2022, from https://www.schoolreforminitiative.org/download/charrette-protocol/

Schultz, M. (2015, March 6). *The importance of getting to know your students*. Retrieved October 3, 2022, from www.bamradionetwork.com/the-importance-of-getting-to-know-your-students

Seidel, S. (2014). *Keep it real*. Retrieved July 19, 2022, from https://www.youtube.com/watch?v=U4eWKoXN4BQ&t=5s

Shapiro, E. (n.d.). *Tiered instruction and intervention in a response-to-intervention model*. Retrieved October 25, 2022, from http://www.rtinetwork.org/essential/tieredinstruction/tiered-instruction-and-intervention-rti-model

Sinek, S. [@SimonSinek]. (2012, August 6). *A team is not a group of people who work together. A team is a group of people who trust each other*. Twitter. Retrieved July 19, 2022, from Twitter https://twitter.com/simonsinek/status/232556392114974721

Sklad, M., Diekstra, R., De Ritter, M., Ben, J., & Gravesteijn, C. (2012). Effectiveness of school-based universal social, emotional, and behavioral programs: Do they enhance students' development in the area of skill, behavior, and adjustment? *Psychology in the Schools, 49*, 892–909.

Study.com. (n.d.). *How to make a budget: Lesson for kids*. Retrieved October 25, 2022, from https://study.com/academy/lesson/how-to-make-a-budget-lesson-for-kids.html

SurveyMonkey. (n.d.). *Student survey questions that will provide valuable feedback*. Retrieved October 30, 2022, from https://www.surveymonkey.com/mp/student-survey-questions

Sutton, A., Williams, H. M., & Allinson, C. W. (2015). A longitudinal, mixed method evaluation of self-awareness training in the workplace. *European Journal of Training and Development, 39*, 610–627.

Taylor, R. D., Oberle, E., Durlak, J. A., & Weissberg, R. P. (2017). Promoting positive youth development through school-based social and emotional learning interventions: A meta-analysis of follow-up effects. *Child Development, 88*(4), 1156–1171.

Technology & Learning. (n.d.). *Robert Marzano's 9 instructional strategies*. Retrieved October 25, 2022, from http://edtechcoachbw.weebly.com/marzano-instructional-strategies.html

Teacher Toolkit. (n.d.). *Gallery walk*. Retrieved November 7, 2022, from https://www.theteachertoolkit.com/index.php/tool/gallery-walk

Tickled Pink in Primary. (n.d.). *Measurement and data activities*. Retrieved October 25, 2022, from https://www.pinterest.com/tickledpinkinprimary/measurement-data-activities/

Valenzuela, J. (2019a). *How students become ideal teammates*. Retrieved July 19, 2022, from https://www.pblworks.org/blog/how-students-become-ideal-teammates

Valenzuela, J. (2019b). *How to prepare students for explaining their work in public*. Retrieved October 25, 2022, from https://www.pblworks.org/blog/how-prepare-students-explaining-their-work-public

Valenzuela, J. (2019c). *Tips for constructivist teachers*. Retrieved July 10, 2022, from https://medium.com/lifelong-learning-defined-for-peak-performance-in/tips-for-constructivist-teachers-de3bfc40ae1e

Valenzuela, J. (2020). *Getting started with integrating SEL into lessons*. Retrieved August 1, 2022, from https://www.edutopia.org/article/getting-started-integrating-sel-lessons

Valenzuela, J. (2021a). *A simple tool to help teachers regulate their emotions*. Retrieved August 4, 2022, from https://www.edutopia.org/article/simple-tool-help-teachers-regulate-their-emotions

Valenzuela, J. (2021b). *A tool to help students make good decisions*. Retrieved February 20, 2023, from https://www.edutopia.org/article/tool-help-students-make-good-decisions

Valenzuela, J. (2021c). *Building relationships with empathy maps*. Retrieved April 28, 2023, from https://www.edutopia.org/video/building-relationships-empathy-maps/

Valenzuela, J. (2021d). *Ending project-based learning units with a call to action*. Retrieved July 18, 2022, from https://www.edutopia.org/article/ending-project-based-learning-units-call-action

Valenzuela, J. (2021e). *How a simple visual tool can help teachers connect with students*. Retrieved September 8, 2022, from https://www.edutopia.org/article/how-simple-visual-tool-can-help-teachers-connect-students

Valenzuela, J. (2022a). *A simple effective framework for PBL*. Retrieved July 18, 2022, from https://www.edutopia.org/article/simple-effective-framework-pbl

Valenzuela, J. (2022b). *A simple tool for aligning instruction and assessment*. Retrieved October 25, 2022, from https://www.edutopia.org/article/simple-tool-aligning-instruction-and-assessment

Valenzuela, J. (2022c). *Boosting critical thinking across the curriculum*. Retrieved October 25, 2022, from https://www.edutopia.org/article/boosting-critical-thinking-across-curriculum

Valenzuela, J. (2022d). *How to give teachers better feedback*. Retrieved October 30, 2022, from https://www.edutopia.org/article/how-give-teachers-better-feedback

Valenzuela, J. (2022e). *Raising equity through SEL: A framework for implementing trauma-informed, culturally responsive teaching and restorative practices*. Solution Tree Press.

Valenzuela, J. (2022f). *Supporting teachers during times of crisis*. Retrieved July 10, 2022, from https://www.edutopia.org/article/supporting-teachers-during-times-crisis

Valenzuela, J. (2022g). *Using frequent feedback cycles to guide student work*. Retrieved October 25, 2022, from https://www.edutopia.org/article/using-frequent-feedback-cycles-guide-student-work

Valenzuela, J. (2022h). *3 ways to activate student engagement*. Retrieved October 25, 2022, from https://www.edutopia.org/article/3-ways-activate-student-engagement

Valenzuela, J. (2022i). *5 key building blocks of effective core instruction*. Retrieved April 30, 2023, from https://www.edutopia.org/article/5-key-building-blocks-effective-core-instruction

Valenzuela, J. (2023). *Using social and emotional learning to guide students from passion to purpose*. Retrieved October 30, 2022, from https://www.edutopia.org/article/sel-students-sense-purpose

Victoria State Government. (2022). *Numeracy for all learners*. Retrieved October 25, 2022, from https://www.education.vic.gov.au/school/teachers/teachingresources/discipline/maths/Pages/numeracy-for-all-learners.aspx

Visible Learning. (n.d.). *John Hattie: "Think of feedback that is received not given."* Retrieved November 6, 2022, from https://visible-learning.org/2013/01/john-hattie-visible-learning-interview/

Waters, S. (2022). *Self-knowledge examples that will help you upgrade to you 2.0*. Retrieved January 17, 2023, from https://www.betterup.com/blog/self-knowledge-examples

Wexley, K. N., Alexander, R. A., Greenawalt, J. P., & Couch, M. A. (1980). Attitudinal congruence and similarity as related to interpersonal evaluations in manager–subordinate dyads. *Academy of Management Journal,* *23*(2), 320–330. https://doi.org/10.2307/255434

Wiglesworth, M., Lendrum, A., Oldfield, J., Scott, A., Ten Bokkel, I., Tate, K., & Emery, C. (2016). The impact of trial stage, developer involvement and international transferability on universal social and emotional learning programme outcomes: A meta-analysis. *Cambridge Journal of Education,* *46*, 347–376.

Wing Institute. (n.d.). *Evidence-based curriculum.* Retrieved October 25, 2022, from https://www.winginstitute.org/effective-base-instruction-evidence-curriculum

Wolpert-Gawron, H. (2019). *How to find experts for your next PBL unit.* Retrieved July 19, 2022, from https://en.wikipedia.org/wiki/Passion_ (emotion)

Zimmerman, P. (2019). *How emotions are made.* Retrieved August 3, 2022, from https://www.noldus.com/blog/how-emotions-are-made

INDEX

and self awareness, 120–121
and SEL Connections, 165
teacher modeling, 85, 164
update, 85, 164
Engagement strategies, 103, 114
engaging content, 92, 94–95, 140–141
engaging students, 101, 103
English Language Learners. *See* ELLs

Fear, 28–31, 61. *See also* Emotions, primary
Feedback
classroom, 166
cycles, frequent, 4, 53, 56–57, 61
importance of, 56
Feelings, 28, 30–32, 36, 51, 80, 85, 91,
159–160, 164–165. *See also* Emotions

Gaming, 107–108
Graphic organizers, 50, 52, 82–83, 109, 162

Hattie, J., 25, 45–46, 57–58, 77, 103–104.
See also Visible Learning
Hooks, compelling, 15, 17, 71, 82, 95,
107–108, 112
HQPBL (High-Quality Project-Based
Learning), 10, 16–17, 20
Hurst, B., 77–78
Hurst, S., 43

Jigsaw protocol, 127
Joy, 28, 29, 30, 31. *See also* Emotions, primary

Language, appropriate, 70, 81, 89, 150,
157, 160
LER (Lucas Education Research), 1, 11–12
Listening, 25, 29, 46, 69–70, 149–50
to feedback, 69, 149
LMS (learning management system), 19, 109

Models of change, 70–71, 73–76,
149–51, 154–158
MTSS (multi-tiered system of supports).
See Tiers
Multimedia, 69, 93, 108, 139, 151
Murals, 78–82, 86–89, 160–161, 166–169
design, 80–82, 86–88, 90, 141, 160–161,
166, 168–69
process, 81, 89, 160, 167, 170

Narratives, 79, 82, 84, 159, 162
National Core Arts Standards. *See* NCAS

National School Reform Faculty. *See* NSRF
NCAS (National Core Arts Standards), 79–80
NSRF (National School Reform Faculty), 61

Passion, 67–74, 76, 90, 99, 149–55
projects, 14, 108, 110, 112
and interests, 68, 70, 72, 149–50, 152–53
to purpose 5-step organizer, 71–73, 76,
90, 99, 150, 152–53
Peace, inner, 29–31
Personal experiences, 43, 79–82, 159, 161–163
Plutchik, R., 29–30
PMIEF (Project Management Institute
Educational Foundation), 16
Polling, students, 37, 45–46, 137,
147, 158, 170
Presenters, 46, 49, 61–62, 136
Problem solving, 12, 38, 44, 91, 110, 119, 121
Professional learning, 46, 133
Professions, 1–2, 118, 174
Programmers, 48–49, 117
Programs, 17–18, 27, 48, 50, 60, 63
Pros, 94–96, 139, 141–43. *See also* Cons

Questions
guiding, 72, 76, 89, 99, 144, 152, 167
student-generated, 108

Reflection, class, 96, 98, 142, 144, 164
Relationship skills, 24–26, 30–31, 38

Sadness, 29, 30, 31. *See also* Emotions, primary
Scaffolding, 128
School Reform Initiative. *See* SRI
Self-management, 5, 19, 24–26, 30–31, 38
Shared agreements, 6, 19, 112, 115, 118–121
Single-point rubrics. *See* SPRs
Software developers, 48–49, 117
Special interests, 14, 108, 110–112, 114
SPRs (single-point rubrics), 58–59, 61,
76, 90, 99
SRI (School Reform Initiative), 61
Standards. *See* Content standards; CCSS
(Common Core State Standards);
CS Standards
Surprise, 28, 29, 30, 31. *See also*
Emotions, primary
Surveys, 22–23, 94, 98, 139, 144–145
student, 13, 37, 45–46, 104, 107, 137, 147,
158, 170. See also Polling, students
teacher, 2, 13

Keep learning...

KEYNOTES & CONSULTING AVAILABLE

A Simple, Effective Framework for Infusing SEL into PBL

Teachers trying their hand at project-based learning (PBL) may be uncertain about strengthening their project ideas and making them the best possible learning experiences for students with diverse social and emotional learning (SEL) needs. This session provides a research-informed framework for getting started with PBL, plus strategies for defining and organizing the student experience that considerably improve academic and SEL outcomes. Participants will discover how the Getting Started With Project-Based Learning Framework can provide elements like empathy, feedback protocols, and emotional intelligence skills that educators can adapt to create the conditions for learning to stick and continue after projects.

Using PBL to Boost Academic, Social, and Emotional Learning

In this extended professional learning workshop, teachers take an action research approach to learning how they can leverage the power of PBL to assist students in developing deeper learning of academic and SEL skills. By engaging in learning walks and a high-level data debrief, participants will learn to use the Getting Started With Project-Based Learning Framework to provide learners with relevant academic and SEL skills that are unique to the needs of their school.

Visit corwin.com to learn more

JORGE VALENZUELA

Jorge Valenzuela is a nationally recognized performance and education coach, author, and speaker at Lifelong Learning Defined. He has helped countless educators improve their leadership and instructional innovation skills. Jorge specializes in emphasizing core instruction and is a trusted deliverer of reputable professional training in team building, PBL, STEM pathways, and SEL integration across the curriculum. Jorge has authored several books and is the host of the Lifelong Learning Defined podcast. You can find him on Instagram (jorgedoespbl) and Twitter (@JorgeDoesPBL).

A Sage Company

CORWIN HAS ONE MISSION: to enhance education through intentional professional learning.

We build long-term relationships with our authors, educators, clients, and associations who partner with us to develop and continuously improve the best evidence-based practices that establish and support lifelong learning.